FORTEN THE SAILMAKER

PIONEER
CHAMPION OF
NEGRO RIGHTS

OTHER BOOKS BY ESTHER M. DOUTY

The Story of Stephen Foster
Ball in the Sky, The Story of John Wise, America's
                Pioneer Aeronaut
Patriot Doctor, The Story of Dr. Benjamin Rush
America's First Woman Chemist, The Story of Ellen H. Richards
Under the New Roof, Five Patriots of the Young Republic

FORTEN
THE
SAILMAKER

PIONEER
CHAMPION OF
NEGRO RIGHTS

by Esther M. Douty

ILLUSTRATED WITH PHOTOGRAPHS

RAND McNALLY & COMPANY   Chicago   New York   San Francisco

For

LOU ANN DOUTY

My favorite librarian

2/13ᵏ

Contents

Acknowledgments

It has been truthfully said that a writer's life is often a lonely one. Yet the writer who is at the same time a researcher enjoys a happier situation. She is aided in her work by intelligent, courteous, efficient, friendly, and stimulating people. In my search for what frequently seemed to be missing pieces of a jigsaw puzzle that could be put together to form the life of James Forten, I was particularly fortunate in the encouragement and skilled guidance that many persons gave to my project.

I am most indebted to Mrs. Dorothy Porter, Librarian of the Negro Collection at the Howard University Library, whose extensive knowledge of Negro history in America was truly "a lamp unto my feet."

My deepest thanks go also to Mrs. Eileen Donahue, a Senior Reference Librarian at the Library of Congress, whose good cheer, scholarship, and energy in tracking down obscure material in that vast institution were far above and beyond the call of duty.

I am especially grateful to Mrs. Miriam C. Daugherty of Radnor, Pennsylvania, who patiently examined hundreds of records of the city of Philadelphia and of the Friends Historical Library at Swarthmore College to turn up important pieces in the James Forten puzzle.

My appreciation goes also to Mrs. Bourgeois of the staff of the New Bedford, Massachusetts, library for her help in my study of the Paul Cuffe papers on deposit there.

To Mrs. Lillian Tonkin of the Library Company of Philadelphia, to Dr. William J. Morgan, Senior Civilian Historian of the United States Navy, to the staffs of the Boston Public Library, the Historical Society of Pennsylvania, the American Philosophical Society, the Schomburg Collection of the New York City Public Library, and of the Cornell University Library, I again say: "Thank you for your interest and assistance."

A final word of gratitude goes to Mr. and Mrs. Thomas Porter of Westport, Massachusetts, who spent considerable time and effort driving me over rough terrain to the sites of Paul Cuffe's home, shipyard, church, and school.

The illustrations are published with the permission of the following institutions: pages 22, 34, and 37, U.S. Navy; pages 75, 76, 78, 96, and 124, Historical Society of Pennsylvania; page 84, Mariners Museum, Newport News, Va.; page 111, New Bedford Whaling Museum and Historical Society; page 187, Boston Public Library (George M. Cushing, photographer). All pictures not specifically cited are from the collections of the Library of Congress.

—Esther M. Douty

List of Photographs

1

At the School of the Small Quaker

All his life James Forten had noticed the sails. The other boys crowded the wharves along the Delaware River, and as they scrambled amid the casks and boxes, the drays, and the burly stevedores, they stared at the ships. The boys knew the name of each one—the great war frigates, the smaller brigs and sloops, the fast cutters, and the sturdy, high-masted merchantmen.

Eight-year-old James recognized the ships as well as his friends did, but it was the sails that took his eye. He loved their gleam in the sunlight, their crack and snap in the wind. He delighted in their look of great white birds gracefully flying in the distance.

James's father, Thomas Forten, who was a sailmaker in the famous Philadelphia sail loft of Robert Bridges, had no such poetic views of sails. "They are just great big pieces of canvas," he told James one day as they stood on the Pine Street landing near Mr. Bridges' sail loft, "but they've got to be made of the best material and sewed together in the strongest way. You don't hear much about it, James, but in a storm the safety of the ship may depend upon the strength of its sails. I don't believe any ship anywhere has ever gone down because of its sails, if they were made in our loft."

There was a note of pride in Thomas Forten's voice when he spoke of his work. He was a tall, well-built man of medium-brown complexion whose father, a slave, had worked so hard for wages "after slave hours" that he had been able to buy not only his own freedom, but his wife's as well.

Thomas Forten's grandfather had been brought from Africa to Philadelphia in a slave ship, but Thomas had never known any of his grandparents. Now, in 1774, he was thankful that he and his wife Sarah both had been born free. Surely, he thought, their children, James and Abigail, with two free-born parents, would never be slaves.

One of Thomas Forten's fondest hopes was that James would also become a sailmaker in Robert Bridges' sail loft, for Mr. Bridges was known to be fair to everyone. Of the forty sailmakers employed there, nearly one-fourth were Negro. The only comment that Mr. Bridges ever made about this situation was that black or white, a man had to do the best kind of work or he would lose his job.

Occasionally Robert Bridges made tents as well as sails. Years earlier Thomas Forten had stitched several pieces of canvas for the tents that Mason and Dixon used in the Pennsylvania wilderness while surveying their famous line.

Thomas Forten had strong, skillful fingers, and James had inherited them. At the age of eight he was known as one of the best marble players in the Penn Street neighborhood where he lived with his parents and sister in a tiny wooden house not far from the Delaware River.

Usually James would get up a game of marbles with some of the boys who hung around the wharves, but on one special sunshiny-golden morning in September, 1774, he had no time for marbles. Over the breakfast scrapple his father had told him to come to the loft because two of the youngest apprentices were sick, and the workmen needed a sharp, clever lad to help out with the needles.

As James hurried over the cobblestones, he noticed a special air of excitement in the streets. In front of the Three Jolly Sailors Tavern stood a noisy crowd of men, mostly ropemakers, sailmakers, sailors, and draymen. He caught the words "Continental Congress" and "trouble with England," but he had no idea what they meant.

When he reached the south wharves where Robert Bridges' sail loft was located, he saw Mr. Thomas Willing standing on the dock, frowning as he studied a document he held in his hands. Thomas Willing was a great man in Philadelphia. For years he had been the city's mayor and the business partner of the wealthy banker and merchant Robert Morris. His fortune in wharves, warehouses, ships, houses, importing and exporting enterprises was considered one of the greatest in the colonies.

Since the Bridges sail loft occupied the whole second floor of one of the Willing warehouses, James often saw the wealthy shipper attending to his business interests on the docks. Occasionally, Willing's son, Thomas Jr., who was the same age as James, came with his father to the wharf, and the two boys played a fast game of marbles. James always won, but Thomas Jr. never seemed to mind. Today, however, Mr. Willing did not have his young son with him. After a quick look at the ships rocking gently in the river, James dashed up the stairs to the sail loft.

As always, the loft floor was smooth as glass and shining clean. It had to be that way. Otherwise the sailmakers might get splinters in their hands when they laid the canvas on the floor to cut it.

James's father was not skilled enough to be a sail-cutter. This job Mr. Bridges usually reserved for himself or for a special few of his highly trained workmen. Thomas Forten was, however, particularly good at sewing the rope to the edges of the sails, a task that required strong, supple fingers.

When James came over to him, his father was seated on his sailmaker's bench, which was mainly a long, heavy wooden plank with holes in one end. The holes contained the sailmaker's tools—the fids of hard hickory wood, the sheath knife, the heavers, the prickers, the marlinspikes, and the thick, three-cornered needles. On the floor beside the bench lay a ball of waxed twine, which is the sailmaker's thread.

"You are in good time, James," his father told him. "We are getting low on needles."

In a sail loft the needles are always kept threaded to speed up the work. James picked up the twine and began pushing it through the large eyes of the needles. He knew exactly how long to make the thread—just the length of his father's arm. A sailmaker's thread was always fitted to his arm because, as he sewed, the thread was thrown back. If it dangled, it got in his way.

While James was threading the twine through the big needles, Mr. Bridges watched him. Bridges was a small, neatly made man, about forty-five years old, with bright blue eyes and black hair mixed with gray. He nodded approvingly.

"After you catch up with the needles, lad," he said, "would you give us a hand with waxing the thread? We're running low on that, too."

"Indeed I will, sir," James answered promptly. He never felt shy around Mr. Bridges, chiefly because his father's employer always seemed kind and friendly.

The wax was not quite ready for him when he carried the balls of twine over to the waxing table. Actually, James thought, he could have made the special sailmaker's wax himself, for he had twice watched it being made, and he learned quickly. One took some rosin, a little tar, some tallow, and a large amount of clear beeswax, and put them all together in an iron kettle. The mixture was then heated and stirred. When it was all melted together, it was dumped into cold water, cooled, and shaped into a waxy ball.

Some sailmakers dipped their twine into tar containing a little oil, but Robert Bridges used only the best material for his sails, and waxed his twine exactly as it was done in the British Navy.

Rubbing the wax carefully all over the twine was a tiring

job. After awhile James stopped to stretch and wiggle his fingers. Then he picked up the ball of wax again and rubbed until his aching arms and fingers forced him to stop. Mr. Bridges saw him hunching and unhunching his shoulders and came over to him.

"You'd best quit now, lad," he said kindly. "You've worked as hard as a fourteen-year-old. Could ye come in tomorrow if Billy and Dick are still sick? There'll be an extra shilling in your father's wages this week, if you do."

James glanced inquiringly toward his father. Thomas Forten shook his head as he spoke. "Thank you, sir, for asking him, and the shilling would be welcome. But tomorrow James goes to school, to Mr. Benezet."

"Mr. Benezet. Well!" Mr. Bridges stared at James, clearly impressed.

Anthony Benezet was one of Philadelphia's greatest men —great in goodness and great in love. Sometimes it seemed that there were as many stories of the little Quaker's nobility of heart, soul, and mind as there were people in the city.

A fellow Quaker told how one morning he had called on Anthony Benezet and found him near the brick kitchen behind his house. Benezet was throwing bread to a large pack of rats that had gathered around his feet like a flock of chickens.

"Why on earth are you feeding these pernicious vermin?" the friend had asked. "They should be destroyed."

"Nay," Benezet had replied, "I will not treat them so; you make them thieves by mistreating and starving them, but I will make them honest by feeding them." And back he had gone to his bread-tossing.

Other Philadelphians remembered that, in 1755, when the British expelled from Canada all French Acadians who would not swear allegiance to the British Crown, many of these refugees landed in Philadelphia hungry and destitute. Their situation was desperate until Anthony Benezet came to

Anthony Benezet and some of his pupils (from an engraving)

their aid. He gathered food, medicine, and clothing for them, and he got them started on work projects until they could support themselves. Under his guidance some made wooden shoes and others manufactured linsey-woolsey cloth. To obtain the material for this coarse cloth the Acadians gathered rags from the streets of Philadelphia and carefully washed and otherwise prepared them.

Although Benezet "looked upon the globe as his country and considered all mankind as his brother," it was natural that he should have a special sympathy for these exiled French people, for he was a member of a French Huguenot family that had been driven out of France for religious reasons.

When he was eighteen—small, thin, and big-nosed—Anthony, who had been living first in Holland and then in England, had come to Philadelphia, where he joined the Quakers and became a teacher and a printer. He used both of these professions for the rest of his life to help and defend all oppressed classes and persons—particularly the Negroes.

He taught in a boys' academy near Germantown, and this was a full-time job, but he would get up before dawn to write letters, articles, and pamphlets against slavery. These he printed and distributed all over America and England without charge. Wherever they were read, the pamphlets had great influence. In England, the noted humanitarians William Wilberforce, Granville Sharp, and Thomas Clarkson declared that the writings of this Philadelphia Quaker had brought them into the fight against slavery. In America, it was Benezet who spurred both Benjamin Franklin and Dr. Benjamin Rush into forming the first abolitionist society.

Benezet was especially interested in improving the condition of the free Negroes, something most people paid little attention to. If the free Negroes were to take care of themselves, he reasoned, they would have to be educated—but therein lay the problem. So far as he knew, no schools or teachers accepted black children.

Benezet decided to teach them himself. In 1750 he opened a free evening school for Negro children in his own home. He felt rewarded as they crowded into his house, their black faces shining in the dim light of the candles as they pored over their lessons.

Interested Philadelphians were amazed by the children's proficiency, but Benezet took their accomplishment as a matter of course. "I can with truth and sincerity declare," he wrote later, "that I have found amongst the Negroes as great a variety of talents as among a like number of whites."

Benezet's evening school soon overflowed his house. His wife complained that there was nowhere for her to sit. Benezet agreed that his dark scholars did need more room and set about raising money from the Quaker Societies in America and England for a school building for the Negro children. In 1770 the school was ready, and the doors were opened to Negro girls as well as to boys. But teachers were hard to find, and on many mornings Benezet himself taught the colored children.

No one knows today just how James Forten came to attend Anthony Benezet's school, which was for a time located in Willing's Alley near the splendid Willing mansion. Perhaps Mr. Willing, who had remarked what a bright lad James appeared to be, personally spoke to Mr. Benezet. Perhaps James himself, playing about the wharves, attracted Mr. Benezet's notice—for James was a fine-looking boy, tall for his age, well proportioned, with proud features, a healthy, chestnut-colored complexion, and large dark eyes shining with intelligence.

Certainly the two must have seen each other, for the small Quaker came often to the wharves to talk to the slaves who stopped there while traveling with their masters, or worked at rugged tasks along the waterfront.

In James's mind, Mr. Benezet on these visits always looked the same: a thin, little man in a long gray cloak, with a large gray hat covering most of his long gray hair. But under the turned-down brim of the hat the eyes were bright and keen, and in his movements Mr. Benezet was almost as quick and lively as James himself.

On the morning that James was to start school, his mother served pop-robbins for breakfast. Ordinarily James loved these dumplings made of flour and eggs and then dropped into boiling milk, but this morning he was too excited to eat. He kissed his mother and sister Abigail good-by and hurried out into the bustling streets.

When he reached the school, a strange sight greeted him. Mr. Benezet had not yet come, but a number of pupils were there, laughing and pointing to the teacher's desk, upon which was a miniature pillory with a living mouse in it. On the pillory hung a sign that one of the older boys read to James:

I stand here, my honest friends
For stealing cheese and candle-ends.

"What do you suppose Mr. Benezet will do?" James asked.

"Sh-h-h, here he comes." The boys muffled their giggles, but they couldn't hide their expectant faces as the teacher stepped into the room. He immediately perceived the unfortunate mouse struggling to withdraw its head and paws from the holes of the pillory.

For a moment he stared in silence. Then he exclaimed, "Poor thing, and who put thee there?"

His keen eyes glanced over the room and saw the guilt on the faces of two of the older pupils.

"Stand on thy bench, lads," he requested in mild but firm tones. While the boys, looking sheepish, stood up before the class, Benezet said, "Oh, this poor mouse may have taken cheese and candles without leave, for which most people would have deprived it of its life, but these two boys more compassionately put it in this confinement."

He carefully lifted the frightened mouse from the pillory and put it outside the door. "Go, poor thing, go," he murmured sympathetically. Then he turned to the two boys and said, "Since thee hast merely imprisoned the mouse instead of killing it, thy punishment will be simply to stay after school and write ten times the verse:

Just be thy thoughts, and all thy words sincere;
And know no wish but what the world may hear.

This kindness of Benezet's heart touched a similar spring of feeling in James Forten. The eight-year-old boy was immediately drawn to the sixty-one-year-old man. He resolved to pay strict attention to every word the small Quaker said and to be as much like him as he could.

One sunny morning about a year later James, on his way to school, paused to watch a new sign being hung over a tavern. He had always liked the gay, bright-colored signs. Now, since he could read, he enjoyed them even more. This one had pictures of a tree, a bird, a ship, and a mug of ale on it. Beneath the pictures James read:

> *This is the tree that never grew.*
>
> *This is the bird that never flew.*
>
> *This is the ship that never sailed.*
>
> *This is the glass that never failed.*

The tavern signs were easy for James to read. In fact, now he could read anything Mr. Benezet put before him, from the Bible to an occasional newspaper. The first month he was in school he learned to read all Mr. Benezet's easy lessons, such as:

> *The bee and the bat*
> *The fox and the cat*
> *A sow and a pig*
> *A nut and a fig.*

Or:

> *The cup and the tea*
> *The gun and the key*
> *A fly on an egg*
> *An ape on his leg.*

Or:

> *Now the sun is set*
> *And the cow is put up*
> *The boy may go to bed.*
> *My son, do no ill.*

He also pleased the schoolmaster by quickly learning to

do most of the sums in his arithmetic book, *Dilworth's Assistant*. His penmanship, too, brought a satisfied look to his teacher's face. Penmanship, in 1775, was almost an art, and all the Quaker schoolmaster's students were required to devote many tedious hours to its practice.

On this particular morning, when James reached the school he handed his copybook of religious maxims to Mr. Benezet. The schoolmaster turned the pages and gazed intently at the clear, round script.

"James," he said admiringly, "thy handwriting is as clear as an engraver's. I shall send it to England so that the Friends there may use it to prove how well a colored child can write, when schooled."

He certainly was having a happy day, James thought at recess, as he pocketed a beautiful blue- and red-striped glass marble he had won in a marble game. Then, just as the State House clock was striking class time again, he saw his sister Abigail running up the street toward him. She was crying.

"James," she wailed, "Ma wants you home quick. Pa fell into the river off a boat, and he's terrible bad off."

When James got home, his father was dead.

There was no one left now to look after his mother and Abigail—no one except himself. The next week he started looking for work. He never went back to Mr. Benezet's, and he never went to school any more at all.

2

Hard Times

James Forten was disappointed that Mr. Bridges couldn't take him on at the sail loft, but at nine years of age he was too young for an apprenticeship. For awhile he was a helper to a chimney sweep and ran through the streets crying, "Sweep Oh! Sweep Oh!" When his employer found a sweep job, James would climb up inside the whole length of the chimney, scraping and brushing down the soot as he went. It was dirty, disagreeable work. He was thankful when Mr. Benezet helped him find a steady job in a grocery store.

He took pride in keeping the store swept and scrubbed and in stacking the barrels of flour and molasses and the boxes of tea and sugar in a neat row behind the counter. Every afternoon he carried groceries to the homes of nearby customers who were not able to call for them. Every evening, after his employer closed the store, James laid cold wet cloths over the vegetables to keep them fresh.

When he was not working at the grocery, James could usually be found somewhere along the river, either on the busy docks or out where the water flowed quietly between tree and meadow. Like most Philadelphians of his day, he was very fond of oysters. Sometimes, especially after a rain, he dug them from the Delaware, succulent and fat. More often he went fishing with a pole and brought half a dozen silvery fish to hook. These, along with the oysters, he took home to his mother who fried them in cornmeal for the evening's meal.

On a hot day the boy liked to go swimming. As his lithe brown body sped gracefully through the water, people marveled at his skill. "He's like a fish himself," they said.

When the weather was too cold for swimming, he often played marbles with some of the other boys who hung around the wharves. Every month the small canvas marble bag that he kept beneath his bed bulged fuller with the choice blood alleys and aggies he had won in games.

James's fondness for marble playing did not please his mother, about whom little is known except that she was "an energetic, hardworking woman with a fine mind." She preferred that he spend his time reading the Bible. This was not only because she wanted her son to know the teachings of the Holy Book, but because she was afraid that after he left school he would forget how to read.

She need not have worried. James was one of those boys who automatically read every bit of print their eyes fall upon. Shop signs, shipping news, store labels, newspapers when he could find them—all these James devoured with his eyes. He regularly practiced his handwriting on the slate Mr. Benezet had given him on his last day at school, and the older he grew, the more like the engraver's art his handwriting became.

The part of his job that James liked best was the delivering. He liked being able to see and hear what was happening on the streets and at the waterfront. Many things that he saw and heard he did not understand, such as the agitated talk— on the streets, on the docks, in front of the taverns—about the unfair way in which Britain was treating its American colonies.

In May of 1775 James noticed numbers of important-looking men, strangers in the city, going in and out of the State House. They were delegates to the Second Continental Congress, his employer told him. They were meeting to decide what the American colonies, acting together, could do to secure just treatment from the British.

One of the Pennsylvania members of this Congress was

Thomas Willing who, James thought, looked worried as he visited his great warehouses on the wharves.

Perhaps this worried look was due to the fact that fewer and fewer ships now rocked at the docks on the Delaware. The vessels were being kept away—not only from Philadelphia, but from all American harbors—by armed British vessels that prowled the coast. As a result, goods of all kinds grew scarce. In June, when the Continental Army was established, its commander-in-chief, General George Washington, had a hard time getting ammunition for the army's guns.

To fight this British menace on the seas, the Continental Congress authorized the building of four small frigates. The Americans were dismayed. Four small ships against the mighty British Navy? It seemed a hopeless venture, but the colonists built the ships anyway.

The first of these frigates, the *Alfred*, spread its sails down the Delaware toward the ocean on a cold, wind-whipped

The only existing actual picture of the frigate Alfred

day in December, 1775. Nine-year-old James Forten, standing amidst the crowd of cheering Philadelphians, stared at the strange flag flying from the mast of the little ship. The flag, which had been hoisted by a young lieutenant named John Paul Jones, bore thirteen red and white stripes and a picture of a rattlesnake ready to strike. Beneath the rattlesnake appeared the words, "Don't Tread on Me."

"Don't tread on me," James repeated to himself, "or I'll strike." He was interested in mottoes, and he wanted to think about this one.

About six months later, on the sunny afternoon of July 8, 1776, James was delivering a sack of cornmeal to an old lady on Pine Street when the bell in the State House tower rang out loud and urgently. Immediately people ran toward the State House Yard. James, without a thought of the old lady's supper, ran with them. Very shortly a man, standing on a raised platform, began to read aloud from the document he held in his hand. The crowd listened with hushed attention.

An excited tremor crept into the man's voice as he neared the end of the document. For a moment he paused, gazed into the faces of the crowd and proclaimed, "We, therefore, the Representatives of the United States of America . . . do, in the Name and by Authority of the good People of these Colonies, solemnly publish and declare, That these United Colonies are, and of Right ought to be Free and Independent States; that they are Absolved from all Allegiance to the British Crown, and that all political connection between them and the State of Great Britain, is and ought to be totally dissolved. . . ."

"And," the man was almost shouting now, "for the support of this Declaration, with a firm reliance on the protection of divine Providence, we mutually pledge to each other our Lives, our Fortunes and our sacred Honor."

At his final words, happy, deafening cheers echoed across the yard. The bell in the State House tower pealed joyously. People tossed their hats into the air.

James timidly touched the arm of the plump Quaker who stood next to him. "Can you tell me, sir," he asked, "why the people are cheering?"

"Gracious, boy," the Quaker said, peering down at him in surprise, "dost thee not know that thee hast just heard the first public reading of the Declaration of Independence of these United States of America? 'Tis an occasion thee will remember with pride all thy life."

"The Declaration of Independence." James had little idea what this meant, but he did know that he had already taken too much time from his work. He trotted off toward Pine Street with the bag of meal bobbing on his shoulder.

The first year of American independence made life harder for James and his family, as it did for most people in the war-gripped nation. Prices soared as goods of every kind grew scarcer. Wool and linen, when they could be found, cost three times as much as they did before the war. When salt was brought in from Bermuda, no matter how high the price, people pushed and jostled each other to get a little of it. Often the grocery store where James worked opened with its bins empty of coffee and sugar and even of flour. Fewer and fewer sleds brought cut logs into the city. The Fortens, together with hundreds of other Philadelphians, scoured the waterfront for driftwood to burn in the fireplace.

But in spite of the hardship, Philadelphia celebrated the first anniversary of the Declaration of Independence with great display and joy. James remembered it as a happy, noisy time. All day long bells rang joyously. Promptly at one o'clock, the ships in the harbor, with gay streamers flying, fired thirteen deafening salutes. At night fireworks blazed in the sky, and almost every householder burned a candle in each window of his home. James and Abigail, with a number of white and Negro companions, raced excitedly through the streets, their faces bright with the gladness they saw everywhere about them.

This gladness was short-lived. Before the month was up,

Philadelphians heard that Sir William Howe intended to attack their city. Soon frightened eyes observed the British fleet at Cape Henlopen, only a short sail away. This report started a rush within the city itself. To eleven-year-old James Forten's eyes all now became hurry, confusion, and noise. The London Coffee House was crowded with people flocking there for news of the approaching British Army. Night and day, wagons loaded with household belongings clattered over the cobblestones as their owners fled from the city to the comparative safety of the countryside. Many shops closed. James, afraid that he would soon lose his job, went to see Robert Bridges, his father's old employer.

Mr. Bridges seemed pleased to see him and asked after his mother and sister, but it was clear that the sail loft was not as busy as James had remembered it. Bridges only shook his head when the boy asked about work there. "The shipping business is on weak legs here, lad," he said. "But when we've won this war, perhaps there'll be an apprenticeship for ye at my loft."

July passed, and Philadelphia baked in the hot August sun, but still the British had not come. Instead, on a quiet Sunday in the middle of the month, ten thousand of General Washington's soldiers marched through the surprised city.

It was a scene that James Forten never forgot. At the army's head rode General Washington himself. By his side, on a fine horse, was the young French general Lafayette, who had crossed the ocean to offer his help to the Americans. In the New England brigades there was a sprinkling of Negro soldiers marching as proudly as the others. Though James was probably too excited to notice, an older observer of the parade wrote that "the troops were ragged. Some had no shoes, and practically none of them wore what might be called an army uniform, but they held themselves proud and straight, and in his hat each soldier wore a sprig of green to give a uniform appearance to their tattered lines. For two days the flags flew, the drums beat rhythmically and the fifes shrilled, 'Yankee Doodle, Keep It Up. Yankee Doodle Dandy.' Hour after hour the city thrilled to the sound of marching feet, the sharp clatter of hooves, and the rumble of the field and siege artillery and the long wagon train."

This march of Washington's men reassured many Philadelphians for a time. Then reports that the British Army was at the city's outskirts again alarmed the city. On the morning of September 26, the dreaded event happened. The British marched into Philadelphia.

James awoke to the blare of warlike music coming from near the State House. He pulled on his clothes and rushed into the street just in time to see the Grenadiers pass by, splendid in their red coats. Behind them were the green-clad Hessians—big, fierce-looking men with long mustaches and gleaming brass helmets—stepping along briskly to the pounding music of their band. All of them, Grenadiers and Hessians alike, looked strong, well fed, and well clad. They appeared to have an endless supply of muskets and cannon. The contrast between them and the poorly equipped American soldiers, who had marched through the same streets a few weeks before, plunged the captured city into gloom.

At first the British occupation made little difference in James's life. Almost none of the people in the poor neighborhood where the Fortens lived had fled the city. They had no wagons to carry their few belongings and nowhere to flee to if they did leave.

At times James still played marbles with his friends, but often now he played a more dangerous game. He joined a group of older boys to fight regular battles against the drummer boys and other youths who were attached to the British Army. As eleven-year-old James was tall, quick, and exceptionally strong, the town boys insisted that he take part in these fights. But one day a drummer boy was killed by a tossed rock, and the British authorities forbade all such bat-

New Market, in South Second Street, Philadelphia, near
James Forten's birthplace, at the time he lived there

tles under threat of severe punishment. Actually James was
glad these street fights were stopped. He did not like to fight
and hurt people.

He still enjoyed studying the ships and their sails, even
though most of them now flew the British flag. One day he
counted sixty British vessels moored so close to each other
in the Delaware that there seemed hardly room for his hand
to pass between them. Three days before the British had entered the capital, James had watched all the American vessels
sail quietly out of the Delaware, headed for some other port
where, for the time being, they would be safe from the enemy.

Unfortunately, the American ships were not safe for long.
In bitter-cold, predawn blackness, one November morning in
1777, British warships trapped most of the little Continental
fleet at Gloucester Point and turned their heaviest guns upon
it. One by one the frigates, the sloops, a ship, and two floating
batteries were set afire and abandoned. Four of the American

vessels blew up, killing many sailors, Negro seamen among them. When James got to the store at seven o'clock the next morning, he could see the flames of the burning ships in the still-dark Philadelphia sky.

After that, matters grew even worse for the Americans. January of 1778 was bitter cold, and the snows were heavy. At Valley Forge, only a few miles from Philadelphia, General Washington's men were barefoot, ragged, and hungry. In Philadelphia, the British soldiers lived an easy life in warm houses. They had good clothing and the best of food and wines that could be taken from American farms or shipped from Europe. They had plenty of fun and entertainment, too, for rich Tories who had stayed in the city did all they could to make life pleasant for them.

James often saw the British commander, Sir William Howe, on the street. He was a fine-looking man, six feet tall, and well proportioned, with a dignified and graceful way of bowing to prominent citizens, such as Thomas Willing who, although not a Tory, had remained in Philadelphia to try to protect his ships and warehouses.

Early in February the situation changed for the better for America. France, an old enemy of England, recognized the United States as a nation, signed a Treaty of Alliance with her, and immediately sent a fleet to America. Learning this, the British feared that the French ships would blockade them in Philadelphia. They recalled the easy-going General Howe, and in his place put the big-nosed, short and fat Sir Henry Clinton. In June, 1778, Sir Henry evacuated all the British forces from Philadelphia.

Now once again American ships sailed up the Delaware to Philadelphia. Many of these vessels were privateers—ships owned by private individuals, but armed and commissioned by the government to capture or destroy enemy shipping. When an American privateer captured an enemy ship, both the ship and its cargo were taken into an American port and

sold. The money from this sale, called prize money, was shared by every member of the crew. The captain drew the largest share, and the lowest-ranking member of the crew drew the smallest.

Not all privateers went to sea just for money. Many, for purely patriotic reasons, fought the fast British cruisers that were often sent in squadrons to hunt them down. Frequently a privateer deliberately sank an enemy ship and its cargo instead of capturing it as a prize. Many times the crews of the privateers risked their own lives and that of their ship to protect other vessels from much larger and more powerfully armed British craft. It was primarily the privateers that made the British trade routes unsafe, intercepted military supplies, and brought in desperately needed goods for the American army and the civilians. Without the privateers the Americans might not have won their Revolution.

Philadelphia, as the leading city and capital of the new nation, was one of the chief ports to which the captured ships and their cargo—the prizes of war—were brought for sale. When a prize was sailed into the harbor, people flocked to the waterfront to inspect it. As soon as the prize's cargo was put up for auction at the wharves or at the London Coffee House, hundreds of people gathered to watch the proceedings.

When he could find the time, James Forten joined these crowds. Like most youths, his imagination was easily stirred. His brown eyes shone bright as he listened to the tales of adventure brought back by the privateersmen. The sailors' stories of little fortunes made quickly especially attracted him, for with each passing month the Fortens' situation became more desperate.

All during the winter of 1780—the *hard winter*, people called it—when the ice on the Delaware was nineteen inches thick, frost was five feet deep in the ground, and squirrels were found frozen dead in their holes, the Fortens had shivered in patched clothing worn thin with age. Now, a year later, they were still wearing the same threadbare garments. But buying new clothing was almost impossible. They were paid in Continental money, and a pair of boots cost $600 and a yard of calico, $85. By January, 1781, it took 7,400 Continental dollars to buy what $100 in foreign gold or silver coin would purchase. Since few people had faith in the new American government, it grew harder and harder to find anyone who would accept Continental money.

One day, about this time, Abigail came home from her job as a cleaning woman, shivering and upset because her shoes had fallen to pieces. Fourteen-year-old James looked at his sister's half-frozen feet, and turned to his mother:

"Ma," he begged, "please let me sign on a privateer. I hear the *Royal Louis* is looking for men."

The *Royal Louis* was a very special privateer: Philadelphia's own fast-sailing huntress of the sea, built by the State of Pennsylvania to protect American vessels from the swift British cruisers that lurked outside the harbor.

It was a formidable ship, mounting 22 guns and carrying a crew of two hundred. Its commander was a strong, heavy-set man named Stephen Decatur, Sr., who had bright blue eyes, a large nose, a firm chin, a frank and open expression, and an air of great competence. He had already won wide acclaim as a privateersman, for he had commanded the brigs *Comet* and *Fair American* in their successful attacks on British ships. On the *Fair American's* last voyage she had brought three British merchantmen, four brigs, and a packet into Philadelphia as prizes. It was no wonder that James Forten wanted to join Decatur's crew. He knew that even a cabin boy's share from such a successful voyage would be worthwhile.

Mrs. Forten, however, was reluctant to give her permission. She knew that privateering was dangerous, and James was precious to her. When finally Abigail added her pleas and arguments to her brother's, their mother gave in. James took off immediately for the new privateer.

The mate of the *Royal Louis* seemed glad to sign him on as a powder boy at four dollars a month. He was probably favorably impressed with the youth's manner and appearance. At the time James was nearly six feet tall, well formed, quick, and strong of body. There was a look of directness and keen intelligence in his lustrous brown eyes. His manner was marked by pleasantness, courtesy, and a simple, natural dignity.

The fact that James was a Negro made no difference one way or the other to the commanding officers of the *Royal Louis*, for in 1781 many black sailors were serving aboard American vessels. The *Royal Louis* had already signed on nineteen black seamen. James made the twentieth.

The Negro race was well represented in the American Army also. It had not been that way at the beginning of the Revolution. In those days the Continental Army did not welcome black men. Soon it barred them completely. The commanding officers, including Washington, feared that perhaps Negroes would not make good fighters, and that possibly they would not be loyal to the United States, despite individual Negro heroism in New England. But when the British proclaimed that any American Negro slave who ran away from his master and joined the British Army would be declared free, the Americans realized that to prevent a wholesale desertion of slaves to the enemy, they, too, would have to offer something to the Negro.

Various states used various methods. In some states, such as Rhode Island and Massachusetts, there were a few all-Negro companies. In most states, however, Negroes were integrated into the fighting groups with whites. Toward the end of the Revolution, only South Carolina and Georgia still resisted the enrollment of Negro soldiers. They paid dearly for this policy. Hundreds of slaves escaped to the British lines.

By the time that Cornwallis surrendered to Washington at Yorktown in October, 1781, about 5,000 Negroes had been listed as serving with the American forces. To the surprise of their white officers, they fought with skill and bravery, some with a valor that won especial praise from Lafayette and Kosciusko.

Not long before he enlisted on the *Royal Louis*, James had heard about the Battle of Red Bank near Philadelphia. Here a regiment of blacks from Rhode Island with a white commander, Colonel Greene, was badly defeated by the British. Greene was severely wounded but, the army report said, "the sabres of the enemy reached him only through the bodies of the faithful guard of blacks who hovered over him to protect him, every one of whom was killed."

Whether James had visions of personal heroism is not known today. In any case he had little time to dream about the future, for as soon as the *Royal Louis* had its crew, it prepared to sail.

On July 23, 1781, the sun glistened brightly on the new privateer as it weighed anchor and sailed out of Philadelphia on its first mission. Below deck, James Forten, combination powder boy and ship's boy, was barely able to stow his two cherished possessions, his Bible and a bag of marbles, before he was summoned to the ship's magazine to learn his duties there.

3

Powder Boy on the *Royal Louis*

The wind was fair in Delaware Bay. Soon the *Royal Louis* was standing out to open sea. At noon, James, carrying a tray of food to the officers' quarters, heard the man upon the mast cry, "Sail ho!"

"Where away?" shouted the officer of the watch.

"Dead ahead, sir."

"What's her rig?"

"Looks like a brig of war, sir."

Captain Decatur stared at the vessel through his long spyglass. "English colors," he called tersely. "Set all sail. Pipe all hands to battle stations."

James, his heart quickening, heard the shrill pipe of the boatswain. In a moment the *Royal Louis* was a scene of disciplined activity. Topmen, some armed with muskets, scuttled up the shrouds and ratlines. Other crewmen threw sand on the decks to keep them from becoming slippery with blood.

The courses (lowest sails) were hauled up, and the topgallant sails were clewed down. On the main deck a boarding party with muskets, pistols, pikes, axes, stinkpots, cutlasses, and grapnels in hand stood ready for action. On the gun deck below, the gun crews knocked open the ports, cast the cannon loose, loaded them with ball and grapeshot, and ran them out into firing position. Alongside the cannon, fast-moving seamen placed ramrods, sponges, tubs of water, extra ammunition, and linstocks with their tow matches already smoldering.

A powder boy on an American frigate during the Revolution
(from a romanticized painting of John Paul Jones)

"Hey, boy," a red-haired sailor standing by a cannon yelled to James. "Over here." Young Forten, as he had been instructed, ran over and stood a little behind one of the gun crews, ready to pass along the powder and ball to the gunners.

In the distance he could see a British brig dipping and swaying over the swirling gray water. Soon it was within musket shot of the *Royal Louis*, near enough so that James could recognize it as the *Active* and distinguish the officers from the men. He particularly noticed the captain on the companionway, a big, broad man with a large, gold-laced cocked hat on his head and a speaking trumpet in his hand.

"What ship is that?" bawled the English captain, while

below him on the gun deck his gunners brought their cannon to bear on the *Royal Louis.*

Captain Decatur did not answer the *Active's* captain. Instead he issued a sharp command to his own men. "Give her a broadside."

Instantly a tremendous roar and flash of cannon shook the *Royal Louis.* The great guns jumped back, straining against the ropes that held them. Small jets of smoke curled up from the vents. James coughed as smoke and acrid fumes blew in from the gunports and eddied through the gun deck. Through the murk he saw the flames of the linstocks glowing with a smoky orange glare.

Again the gun crews prepared for action. The sponger rammed a wet sponge down the muzzle to clear it of any burning fragments from the previous firing. James, nearly deaf from the blast, passed another cartridge and cannonball to the loader who rammed them down the muzzle with his ramrod.

Then, as the great guns were being pulled back into the battery for a second broadside, he raced below to the magazine. He found the entrance blocked by a water-soaked screen with a hole in it through which a grimy hand passed him a cannonball and a bag of powder. From above, came the shouts of the men and the crack of muskets. Shielding the powder against the flying sparks with his jacket, the powder boy dashed back to his cannon.

As he ran, the *Active's* big guns spat out their deadly fire. A charge of grapeshot sprayed into one of the privateer's portholes, wounding two men who fell, groaning, to the floor. James, rushing to help them, felt the ship swing sharply; Captain Decatur was maneuvering the *Royal Louis* into position to rake the deck of the *Active* with musket fire. The deadly balls struck the British captain, and he was carried below. The brig's first lieutenant took command. The fight went on.

For an hour the two vessels poured broadside after broadside into each other. The smoke around both ships was so thick that only the flames spewing from the enemy's guns penetrated the murk and showed the gunners where to aim. A cannonball had splintered one of the masts of the *Royal Louis*. Her sails hung in shreds. Dead and wounded men lay on her decks in a tangle of splintered wood and fallen rigging.

There was no letup in the battle. James winced, unaccustomed to the shouted commands, the cries of the wounded men, the smoke, the flames, the fumes, the shock and thunder of the cannon, and the crack of muskets. His eyes stung. His jacket was covered with blood from the wounded men he had tried to help. His arms ached from carrying the bags of powder from magazine to gun crew. Suddenly, with a clash and a shudder of timbers, the two ships banged together.

"There go the grapnels," shouted a smoke-blackened gunner, as the rasp of iron hooks tearing on wood sounded above a brief letup in the firing.

"Boarders away," roared Decatur. The Americans swarmed over the bulwarks and slashed through the boarding netting of the brig. Cutlass rang against cutlass as desperate hand-to-hand fighting began.

James, no longer needed to carry powder to the gun crews, grabbed a boarding pike and dashed to the upper deck. He was just in time to see the privateer's marksmen pick off the men in the main and mizzen topsails of the enemy.

All at once flames burst out at several points on the *Active*. Her fire slackened. A feeble cheer went up from the exhausted crew of the *Royal Louis*. The British ship had struck her colors.

There was not much cargo aboard the *Active*, but Decatur considered the British prisoners far more valuable than cargo. He could use them to exchange for some of the thousands of American prisoners the British held in deadly captivity.

Captain Decatur immediately placed a prize master and

Captain Stephen Decatur, Sr., Commander of the
Royal Louis (from a painting by C. W. Peale)

crew aboard the captured vessel and ordered it to Philadelphia.
The *Royal Louis*, her mast and sails repaired, continued out
to sea. James shared in the general good feeling. Success won
so soon by a brand-new privateer was a good omen, the sailors
said. Surely the *Royal Louis* was a lucky ship.

Toward late afternoon of the next day the privateer fell
in with a brigantine of fourteen guns called the *Phoenix*. The
Phoenix crowded on all sail and proceeded to run away from
the privateer.

"Give chase, lads," Decatur ordered. The *Royal Louis* also crowded on all sail and was gaining on its quarry, when the black clouds of an approaching thunderstorm brought on an early darkness. The *Phoenix* disappeared into the sheltering night.

"She's hereabouts, all right," Decatur said grimly. "Keep watch."

Suddenly, by the flashes of lightning, the lieutenant, his spyglass clapped to his eye, discovered the brigantine standing in a different direction from the one they had expected. The *Royal Louis* shifted its course and pressed on all sail in pursuit. By the aid of the lightning, the privateer kept the *Phoenix* in course and soon came up with her.

"What ship is that, and where from?" roared the captain of *Royal Louis*, as thunder rolled above the raging water.

"The brigantine *Phoenix*, from Charleston, bound to London," was the reply. A flash of lightning showed English colors at the brigantine's mast and at the same moment revealed the American flag at the privateer's masthead.

The American crew was ready for action. Lanterns burned fore and aft. The tow matches were smoldering. Each member of the crew stood at his battle station, alert and waiting for orders.

"Give her a broadside," shouted Decatur.

The *Royal Louis* shook with the thunder of the cannon. A ball smashed into the rigging of the *Phoenix*, but the brigantine's guns remained silent.

"Haul down your colors or we'll blow you out of the water," Decatur yelled through his speaking trumpet.

The *Royal Louis* must have looked invincible, or else the *Phoenix* did not wish to fight, for a moment later a lightning flash revealed the English flag fluttering down in surrender.

Again the Americans cheered, more vigorously than when they had taken the *Active*, for this victory had been quick and easy. A boat with a prize master and crew immediately put out from the *Royal Louis* for the captured vessel. They rejoiced to find that the *Phoenix* carried a rich cargo—rum, coffee, pimento, and tobacco. As soon as the English crew was imprisoned in the hold of the *Royal Louis*, both ships set sail for Philadelphia. At noon the next day they dropped anchor in the harbor amid the loud huzzas of the crowds on the wharves, who were cheered by each small American triumph.

James eagerly asked for permission to hurry home to tell his mother the good news. Soon he was saying jubilantly, "I'll get a nice little share for my part in these captures, Ma. The *Louis* is a lucky ship. Maybe next time we'll take a prize with an even better cargo—guns, perhaps even gold."

But his mother could not share his enthusiasm. "Lucky ship?" she said, tonelessly. "Who knows, James? The next time you may be the cargo."

4

On the
Prison Ship
Jersey

Early in October the *Royal Louis* again prepared to sail. As before, James packed his Bible and his bag of marbles and told his mother and Abigail good-bye. Mrs. Forten was not able to keep the tears from her eyes. She had not wanted James to join the privateer's crew the for the first cruise, but at that time she had not broken down into uncontrolled sobs as she was doing now.

James was distressed by his mother's tears, but he had signed on as powder boy and felt he should keep his agreement. He climbed aboard the privateer in a chill wind. Shortly afterward, the *Royal Louis* weighed anchor, and with her great sails spread, thrust her nose into the heavy swell on Delaware Bay and stood out for the open sea.

All that day and all that night she beat against the wind. Early the next morning the lookout sighted a sail on the larboard quarter. Captain Decatur fixed his glass on the distant vessel, but she was still hull down and only her upper rigging showed. Soon, however, he was able to make out the lower sails. "A ship," he called, "a full-rigged ship."

The crew of the *Royal Louis* looked at one another uneasily. Was the large vessel a merchantman or a warship? As yet no one could tell. Nevertheless Decatur ordered, "Give chase, lads. We'll soon see if this fine ship carries a fine cargo."

About noon a hail from the other ship came faintly across

the water. "This is His British Majesty's frigate, *Amphyon*. What ship is that?"

The *Amphyon*. A man-of-war! James swallowed nervously and looked around at the two Negro seamen who stood near him. Their steady eyes and calm manner gave him courage.

"Hoist American colors. Pipe all hands to battle stations," roared Captain Decatur. "We'll give them a proper fight."

James was running toward his station by the cannon when the lookout called, "Two sail to the leeward."

James glanced in that direction. Even with his naked eye he could make out two large vessels looming over the horizon. Far above his head the lieutenant clung to the main topsail with his spyglass clapped to his eye.

"British ships of the line, sir," he called down to the captain.

Decatur's heavy eyebrows drew together. "We can't take on the three of them. We'll have to make a run for it, lads. Stand back for the bay."

Immediately all hands on the *Royal Louis* ceased their battle preparations and bent their efforts toward helping the privateer escape. They wet their sails and shifted the position of their guns. Then, crowding on all canvas and running dead before the wind, the *Royal Louis* fled from the pursuing warships.

For six hours the chase continued. At noon the wind shifted, and the warships fell into the privateer's wake and gained upon it very fast. Moments later the *Amphyon's* powerful guns blasted out a broadside that tore holes in the privateer's rigging.

"Strike those colors," the British captain boomed through his trumpet, "or we'll blow you out of the water."

Even as he shouted, the two other warships, *Nymph* and *Pomona*, bore down upon the American vessel, the ugly snouts of their cannon poking through the gunports.

Captain Decatur, so fortunate on his earlier cruises, was forced to admit that his ship's position was hopeless.

"Strike." His voice came wearily through his speaking trumpet. The American colors fluttered slowly down in defeat.

Already James could see the enemy boats putting out for the *Royal Louis*. Soon all of them, even the stalwart Captain Decatur, would be prisoners of war. Fear prickled cold along his spine. What would happen to him and to the nineteen other Negro seamen aboard the captured privateer? Negro prisoners, he knew, were seldom exchanged. Instead they were sent in chains to the West Indies to be sold into slavery. They were sold like cargo. Like cargo! James recalled his mother's words. "Next time, maybe you'll be the cargo." His fright grew.

"Show a leg there, boy." One of his shipmates grabbed his arm roughly. "Get your gear whilst ye can. Them— —'ll be aboard in a minute."

James ran for his hammock and snatched up his Bible, some clothing, and his bag of marbles. For the next few minutes all was confusion. He was dimly aware that someone in a British uniform was snarling, "Get down there, you damned rebel," and was pushing him over the side of the *Royal Louis* into one of the enemy boats waiting below.

The crew of the *Royal Louis* was divided so that one-third of the men were sent to each of the three capturing warships. James Forten was one of about a hundred seamen rowed to the largest ship, the *Amphyon*. He lined up with the other captives on the pitching deck of the warship to face the captain's inspection.

Was it his imagination, James wondered, or did the British captain, Sir John Beasly, give him a particularly searching glance? His heart jumped as Beasly asked, "How old are you, boy?"

"Fifteen, sir." Was that a good age for a slave? James wondered, wildly.

Captain Beasly's sharp eyes fell to the small cloth bag James clutched in his hand. "What've you got there?"

"Just marbles, sir." James's face felt warm with embarrassment. Suddenly marbles seemed a childish thing for him to have taken to sea.

"H-mph. I had an idea that's what the bag contained. Well, you're a likely looking lad. Perhaps a game of marbles will be just the thing to lift my Willie out of the doldrums. By the way, what's your name?"

James told him, and Sir John turned his attention to the other prisoners. Later that day, as James sat under guard on the floor of the quarterdeck with his captured shipmates, a sandy-haired boy about his own age approached him.

"You the powder boy from the *Royal Louis?*" the youth asked.

James nodded, while his fellow captives stared.

"I'm William Beasly. My father said you've brought marbles aboard. I'd like a game."

James jumped up and picked some of his most treasured marbles out of his bag. At the sight of the "white alleys and blood-alleys, the striped plasters and bull's eyes, the crystals clear and clouded" Willie Beasly whistled in admiration. James bent down and with a burnt stick drew a ring upon the deck. Then, since William had no marbles of his own with him, young Forten gave him part of his collection.

James won first play. He knuckled down, his favorite taw in his hand. "Crack!" his shooter struck Willie's marble out of the ring. On and on they played while the other prisoners watched silently, not daring to cheer James against the captain's son, and yet not wanting the English boy to win.

Soon James's deft, strong fingers and unerring aim had won all his marbles back for him, but Willie would not let him stop. The English boy's face, glum and depressed when he first spoke to James, already looked more cheerful.

This was the first of many games the two boys played

upon the deck of the *Amphyon*. William Beasly, ever astonished by James's skill and cleverness, became extremely fond of
him as a friend. One day he asked his father if they could take
the bright Negro youth back to England with them and
provide for his education.

Sir John was himself impressed with young Forten. "An
open and honest countenance. Strong, and of excellent intelligence," was the comment he made about James to the
Amphyon's lieutenant.

The fact that James was obviously a superior individual
bothered the British captain. It was true, as James had heard,
that Negroes captured while fighting with the American forces
were sold into West Indian slavery. Sir John disliked to think
of such a fate for the engaging young Philadelphian. On the
other hand, the captain reflected, if James shared the lot of
the other prisoners from the *Royal Louis*, he probably would
be no better off; for although the American captives had not
yet been told, the *Amphyon* was conveying them to the most
dreaded of all British prison ships—the *Jersey*—which lay with
its rotting human cargo off the lonely shore of Long Island.

Sir John pondered the matter for several hours and then
decided to give in to his son's plea. He sent for James to come
to his cabin. When the youth heard what the captain had to
say, he truly didn't know what to answer. Here he was being
offered a chance to live in a fine house with his friend, Willie
Beasly, and to receive a good education, something he and his
mother had dreamed of. Surely he would never have such an
opportunity again. And yet he didn't know. He returned Captain Beasly's gaze uncertainly.

"Come, come, boy." Sir John was impatient, incredulous
that James would hesitate for even an instant. "Surely, you
wouldn't be fool enough to turn aside such a stroke of good
fortune."

"I'm afraid I must, sir," James is reported as saying. "I am here as a prisoner for the liberties of my country. I cannot prove a traitor to her interests."

The British captain was both astonished and angry at Forten's rejection of his offer. Still he could not bring himself to sell the youth into slavery in the West Indies. But now he had no choice, he felt, except to transfer James, along with the other captives, to the prison ship *Jersey*.

The day before James was taken off the *Amphyon*, Willie Beasly ran to him and hugged him tight. He handed young Forten a note. "This is for you, James," he said, with tears in his eyes. "It's from my father. It will help you."

The note was to the commander of the prison ship, informing him that James Forten was "an excellent youth and should not be forgotten on the list of [prisoner] exchanges."

James carefully placed the note in a safe place. "Thus," he remarked often in later years, "did a game of marbles save me from a life of West Indian servitude."

Late the next afternoon the *Amphyon* dropped anchor near the city of New York and signaled that she had prisoners aboard. Soon several large boats came alongside. In one of these was seated the notorious David Sproat, the Commissary of Prisoners, an American Tory who was universally detested for his cruel and insolent manner. His eyes lit with relish at the sight of so many new American prisoners. James was placed in Sproat's boat.

A heavy silence hung over the Americans as their captors rowed them toward the *Jersey*, whose very name struck terror into their hearts. All of them had heard that to be confined within her filthy, slimy hulk was equal to a sentence of death from which there was little hope of escape.

Originally the *Jersey* had been a British ship of the line, a large one, mounting 74 guns. At the beginning of the Revolution, the *Jersey*, an old vessel and much decayed, was dis-

The prison ship Jersey

mantled, moored in the East River, and converted into a store ship. In 1780 she became a prison ship, confining one thousand prisoners at a time. During the three years of her service, more than 11,000 American prisoners died of disease, starvation, and plain maltreatment on board this "hell afloat."

Now as the boat cut slowly through the water, James hardly dared raise his eyes, but a sudden cry from Sproat made him look up. Before them, forbidding and gloomy, lay the dreaded black hulk. "There, rebels," shouted Sproat, pointing exultantly, "*there* is the cage for you."

It was dark when the American prisoners were finally permitted to ascend the accommodation ladder to the upper deck of the *Jersey.* Lanterns were lighted so that the British officials could question and examine each prisoner. Although he handed Sir John's note to the officials, James seemed of no particular interest to them. In a few minutes he was ordered down the hatchway to the main prisoner quarters.

As soon as all the prisoners were gathered below, gratings were placed over the hatchways and fastened down for the night. James felt around for a bare space on the floor. No light was ever allowed the prisoners, and it was impossible to recognize anyone in the darkness so that James felt he was surrounded by strangers about whom he knew nothing except that they were as miserable as he was. From every direction, the groans and wild, delirious ravings of the sick and dying met his ears. A foul, loathsome odor filled his lungs. The stifling heat sickened him.

The thought of sleep did not enter his mind. After awhile he noticed a glimmer of light coming through the iron grating of an air hole. If only he could get near the hole, the youth thought longingly, perhaps he could get one saving breath of fresh air. He began to make his way toward the side of the ship but, with a curse, a prisoner, upon whom he had unwittingly stepped, knocked him to the floor.

For the rest of the dreadful night James lay huddled between the restless, moaning men, anxiously waiting for daylight. When dawn came he found himself amid a collection of the most wretched and disgusting-looking objects he had ever seen in human form. Their bodies were covered with rags and filth. Their faces were pale with disease, emaciated from hunger and anxiety. Their hair was matted and foul. James stared at them in horror, wondering how long it would be before he would look as they did.

At sunrise the prisoners were allowed to ascend to the upper deck where they gratefully gulped the fresh air. James, scrambling up the ladder with the rest, searched through the horde of ragged, dirty, half-starved men for a familiar figure. After awhile he found one—a wiry, freckle-faced boy from Philadelphia named Daniel Brewton, who had also been a ship's boy on the *Royal Louis*.

Daniel was only fourteen, a year younger than James. When he saw the stalwart, brown-skinned Forten, he flung his arms around him and tried to keep back the tears. James's eyes fastened on the silk handkerchief Daniel wore knotted around his neck. It appeared to be alive with crawling black spots.

"Ugh," he cried in disgust, "vermin." He snatched the kerchief from his friend's neck and flung it overboard. Then he felt something crawling on his own head and down his neck and arms. He, too, was covered with the horrible black lice that infested the entire hulk and crept over the helpless men, carrying disease as they went.

James soon learned that vermin were among the lesser horrors of the *Jersey.* Much worse were the drinking water and the food. The water, stored in enormous casks that were never cleaned, was thick and clammy, with a foul odor. The food allowance for the week—what little there was of it—never varied: pork, salt beef, dried peas, oatmeal, flour, biscuit, and "butter."

The biscuit was moldy and filled with worms. The pork was slimy with decay and stank so that even the half-starved prisoners could seldom bring themselves to swallow it. The mahogany-colored beef, completely saturated with salt, was so tough that it had to be cut with an ax. The damaged dried peas were as indigestible as grapeshot. The flour and oatmeal were sour, and the oil and suet, which passed as butter, were rancid.

Even James, with a healthy boy's appetite, ate so little that he lost weight. Daniel Brewton, who did not have James's naturally strong constitution, quickly sickened. Both boys would have given anything for a glass of pure water and some fresh fruit and vegetables.

They tried to keep themselves clean, but it wasn't easy, since no water was provided for bathing or for washing clothes. Soon, like the other prisoners, they threw their garments into the sea, then drew them up and stamped them out upon the deck. For bathing, a soapless rag dampened in the dirty water near the ship had to do.

James could not stand the empty idleness. He volunteered to help wash down the decks or hoist on board the wood, water, and other supplies that were brought to the ship's side. He carried up the sick from the suffocating hold and placed them upon the center deck where they could breathe the fresh air. Often he was ordered to bring up the bodies of the hapless men who had died during the night and place them on the booms—a task that brought tears of pity to his eyes.

Young Forten's cheerful face and helpful nature won him many friends among the prisoners. One of these was an officer in the Continental Navy who confided that he was to be exchanged the next day for a British officer. He asked if James would help carry his sea chest to the boat which was to come for him in the morning.

James's glance went to the sea chest, and his dark eyes brightened. The chest was a large one—large enough for James to hide in. His heart began to beat fast. Would the officer allow him to crawl into the chest during the dark night and be secretly carried off with it in the morning?

The officer agreed, provided that James could manage it when the officer himself was not around to see him crawl in. Then if they were caught, the officer could better plead innocence and perhaps escape severe punishment.

Joy flooded through the youth. Soon he would be off the hated ship. After four months of horror and misery he would again be where water was clean and food was not spoiled, where air was fresh and sweet, and men were not crowded together in a nauseous pit.

He was sitting on the officer's sea chest making final plans for his escape when his friend Daniel Brewton came up to him. Daniel looked dreadful. His face was as white as a sail. His eyelids were red and granulated from lack of proper food. He was covered with sores from the bites of vermin. His ragged clothing hung loosely on his shrunken frame. Too weak to stand long, he flung himself down at James's feet.

Young Forten stared at him and shivered with a chill of foreboding. If Daniel did not get away from the *Jersey* soon, he would die. James did not want Daniel to die. He was only fourteen years old, and, like James, he had a mother and a sister waiting for him at home in Philadelphia, depending upon him.

In an instant James made up his mind. "Quick, Daniel," he said, "you get into the sea chest. I'll see that you get safely off the ship."

The next morning James and the officer carried down "a chest of old clothes" to the boat which had come to carry the exchanged prisoners back to freedom. As the boat disappeared toward the shore James tried to shake off a feeling of gloom. Would he ever get off the *Jersey?* he thought miserably. How much longer could he endure the horrors of the prison ship?

But in a little while he had regained his good spirits. He knew that he had the strength to withstand the torments of the *Jersey* if he had to.

James Forten remained a prisoner on the *Jersey* for three more months, seven months in all. Then, with the Revolution almost over, he was released in a general exchange of prisoners. Without shoes and without a whole piece of clothing to cover his body, he walked the entire distance to Philadelphia. Among other evidences of the great hardships he had endured, his hair was nearly entirely worn from his head.

At the sight of him, his mother and Abigail, who had given him up for dead, shrieked with joy and hugged him close. After he had rested for a few days, he looked up his friend Daniel Brewton and was overjoyed to find him safe and completely restored to health.

Daniel Brewton never forgot what James Forten had done for him. Fifty-six years later Brewton, who in his old age served as Steward of the Philadelphia Lazaretto (Free Public Hospital) told his story to William Nell, an early Negro historian. "With tears raining down his face," Nell wrote, "the old man [Brewton] told how James Forten had saved his life when they were both captives on the prison-ship *Jersey*."

5

James Forten
in England

Not long after James Forten returned home, Britain formally admitted that she had lost the war with her American colonies. In September, 1783, her representatives met in France with the American Peace Commissioners—Benjamin Franklin, John Adams, and John Jay—and reluctantly signed the Treaty of Paris. The long hard struggle was over. The United States of America was a free and independent nation.

To seventeen-year-old James the news provided an opportunity to do something he had been considering ever since Captain Beasly of the war frigate, *Amphyon*, had offered to take him to England for an education. Now that there was peace between the two nations, he determined to go to England himself, work in that country awhile, and see what it was like. If English life appealed to him, he might settle there and live permanently among the English people.

James's chance to go to England came sooner than he expected. His sister Abigail had recently married a sailor named Dunbar who, in the early winter of 1784, signed on as a member of the crew of the ship *Commerce*, which was sailing for Liverpool within a fortnight. The *Commerce* needed several more able-bodied seamen. Dunbar was sure that its captain would be glad to have a nimble, stalwart youth like James aboard.

Dunbar was right. James was immediately accepted for the crew of the *Commerce*. He boarded ship in a sharp February wind and was soon carried away from his native land by a stout, steady breeze that raised a white chop on the sea and heeled the vessel before it.

Four weeks later, the *Commerce* docked at the busy port city of Liverpool, and the crew gratefully hurried ashore. Dunbar, who had been to the English city before, quickly found a room for James and himself in a sailors' lodging house run by a jolly, gray-haired Negro from the West Indies. As soon as his few belongings were stowed in his room, James went for a walk.

He began his stroll at the wharves along the River Mersey's edge. Across from the wharves were numerous stores which serviced the ships and their crews. James paused before one shop and stared into the window. He was not quite sure what he was looking at. The merchandise seemed designed for prisoners. He recognized the leg shackles and the handcuffs, but what were those large screws and those other metal contraptions which somehow made him think of something that would be used to force a horse's mouth open.

While he was puzzling over the objects, a man stopped beside him and also looked into the ship chandler's window. James glanced at him with interest. He thought at once of his beloved schoolmaster, Anthony Benezet. This gentleman must also be a Quaker, James decided, for he wore the customary broad-brimmed hat and the simple gray cloak and suit. Probably because the man was a Quaker, James ventured a question. "What, sir, are those?" he asked, pointing to the strange metal objects in the shop window.

The man gave him a sad look. "Ah, lad, 'tis well thee does not know those strange metal objects. One is a thumbscrew for torturing the poor captured Africans when they do not do what their captors aboard the slave ship tell them. And the other is called a *speculum oris*, a mouth-opener. It is used to force these hapless people to eat when they would rather die than be carried into slavery."

James was silent. A sick, clammy feeling slid down his spine. Of course he knew about slaves. There were many in Philadelphia, and many more from other states who came to the city with their masters. And yet he himself had never felt very close to, or even involved with, these unfortunate beings. He had always felt free, thought free. His parents had been free people—self-reliant, hardworking, respected by other Philadelphians. James himself had always been treated well. He remembered Anthony Benezet and Thomas Willing, Robert Bridges, Captain Decatur and the other crew members aboard the *Royal Louis*, Sir John Beasly of the *Amphyon*. They had all been kind to him, fair, just, and helpful. No wonder that, aside from the brief moment of fear when he was captured aboard the *Royal Louis*, James had never even felt threatened by this evil thing, this man-stealing.

But now somehow for the first time in his life he felt that he was a part of those unfortunate people who were being carried into slavery, that his life was related to those who shared a common heritage with him.

He looked down from his height of six feet two inches and met the sympathetic gaze of the elderly Quaker who suddenly drew a pamphlet from under his cloak and handed it to him.

James gave a start. The pamphlet was entitled "A Caution and Warning to Great Britain and Her Colonies—a Short Representation of the Calamitous State of the Enslaved Negroes in the British Dominions." It had been written by Anthony Benezet.

His companion was watching him. "Ah, thee knows the name of Friend Benezet then."

"He was my schoolmaster, my only one," James said, noting that the pamphlet had been published in 1766, the year he was born.

The Quaker glanced around as though to make sure no one was watching him. Then he quickly drew another pamphlet from under his cloak. This one, entitled "An Historical Account of Guinea—Its Situation, Produce, and General Disposition of Its Inhabitants," had been published by Benezet in 1771.

As James took the booklet into his hand, the Quaker said, "We are organizing a petition to Parliament against the slave trade, and are finding this pamphlet of great use in our labors. 'Tis said that it was these writings of Friend Benezet which inspired Granville Sharp to his great work in the Somersett case."

Granville Sharp. That name too was familiar to James. He seemed to recall Mr. Benezet happily telling his pupils one morning that he had just received a letter from a great friend of theirs in England, Granville Sharp.

Forten impulsively turned the first page and began to read.

"Since thee is fortunate in knowing how to read, lad," the old Quaker's kindly voice interrupted him, "thee may have these pamphlets for thy own. And also this one about Sharp and the Somersett case, which should interest thee mightily."

His new friend left, and James continued his stroll. Tomorrow would be time enough to find a job, he told himself.

By noon of the next day young Forten was working as a stevedore for one of the shipping companies along the Mersey. The English dockworkers pretty much ignored him, but at night he and Dunbar, who was waiting for the *Commerce* to return to America, found companions aplenty in the taverns that abounded in the neighborhood.

In the taverns he learned of matters that upset him and made him unhappy. Perhaps the account that distressed him the most was the one about the slave ship *Zong*.

In 1781, while James was serving his country aboard the *Royal Louis*, the slaver *Zong* sailed from the West Coast of Africa bound for Jamaica, carrying more than four hundred slaves. Early in the voyage, sickness set in, and the captain feared he might lose his entire "cargo." He was beside himself with worry. Then he remembered that according to his insurance policy, the insurance company would bear the loss if the captain were compelled to throw overboard any part of the cargo to save the rest.

Why not, the captain reasoned, put the loss of the sick slaves on the insurance company? To carry out this plan, he told his crew that the ship was short of water, and that the only hope of safety for the majority of the slaves lay in getting rid of some of them. The crew protested slightly, but they followed the captain's orders, brought up on deck one hundred and thirty of the sickest slaves, and drove them overboard into the sea.

James's mouth went dry with horror. "Was nothing done to the captain?" he asked. "Wasn't he put on trial for murder?"

"Oh, yes, he was put on trial," his informant told him, "but not for murder. The court action was only to determine whether the throwing of the slaves overboard was a genuine act of jettison for which the insurance company would have to pay, or whether the captain and the Zong's owners were trying to defraud the insurance company."

After he heard about the slave ship Zong, James wasn't sure he wanted to live in England. He wished he could talk to the old Quaker about his plans, but although he often walked through the ship chandlers' section, searching for the kindly man who had given him the pamphlets, he never saw him again.

The pamphlets he kept, along with his Bible and some plays of Shakespeare he had picked up in a secondhand book store, in a box beneath his bed. At night, long after Dunbar had fallen asleep, James held the pamphlets close to the wavering candle flame and avidly read the small print.

The pamphlet that dealt with Granville Sharp interested

him the most. He read and re-read the account of this remarkable man's activities on behalf of the Negroes, until he could almost repeat them by heart.

Granville Sharp was the twelfth of the thirteen children of the Archdeacon of Northumberland. Although Granville was bright, there was no money for his education. At fifteen he was apprenticed to a linen-draper in London, a job he hated. Fortunately for him the linen-draper went out of business, and Granville was able to secure a minor job in the Government Ordnance Office where the short hours gave him time to study Greek, Hebrew, and the Bible.

One day, in 1765, the thirty-five-year-old government clerk was leaving the office of his brother, Dr. William Sharp, when he met in the street Jonathan Strong, a Negro slave. Jonathan, who was trying to get to the doctor's office, appeared to be dying. Kindhearted Granville lifted the slave in his arms and carried him in to his brother.

As soon as Dr. Sharp had treated the worst of the man's wounds, Granville questioned him. He found that Jonathan was the "property" of David Lisle, a lawyer from Barbados who had brought the youth to England with him. Lisle, ill-tempered and cruel, had beat the boy so often and so savagely that he became weak and lame. One day, in a terrible outburst of rage, Lisle pistol-whipped his slave on the head until the boy became nearly blind. Then concluding that his "property" was so badly damaged as to be useless, Lisle turned Jonathan into the streets to die.

Shocked by the youth's story, the Sharp brothers arranged for him to be admitted to St. Bartholomew's Hospital, where he stayed four months at their expense. When he was well enough to work, they found him a job as an errand boy for a druggist.

One day, two years later, Jonathan's former owner happened to meet him in the street. Lisle observed with surprise that the property he had discarded as useless had regained its value and was being used by someone else. He followed Jonathan to the druggist's house to make sure he could find him again. Then, since he legally still owned Jonathan, he sold him at a reduced price to a Jamaica planter named Kerr, to be shipped to the West Indies. Kerr, to make sure of his bargain, had Jonathan kidnapped and taken to the Poultry Counter prison where the jailor agreed to lock him up until a West India ship should sail.

Jonathan, in despair, sent a message to the man who had once saved his life, and begged his help. Sharp immediately rushed to the prison. He found the terrified slave in an understandable state of panic. Although he had no real authority to do so, Sharp warned the jailor not to give up the prisoner. At the same time he called upon the Lord Mayor to order "all persons who pretended to have any claim on the person of Jonathan Strong to be summoned before his Lordship."

Kerr's lawyer and the West Indian captain who was to take the slave to Jamaica produced Lisle's bill of sale and claimed him as Kerr's property; but the Lord Mayor was not sure that even a slave could be imprisoned unless he was charged with some offense. He ordered Jonathan to be freed.

The slave owners, Lisle and Kerr, were furious. Lisle challenged Granville Sharp to a duel. Sharp laughed at the challenge. Then Lisle, a lawyer, positive that the law was on his side, brought suit for two hundred pounds against the Sharp brothers for depriving him and Kerr of their property.

At this point, most people would have given up the struggle, but not Granville Sharp. He had never opened a law book in his life, but he refused to believe that slaves could legally be held in England. He determined to search through all the laws of England, if necessary, for evidence to support his opinion and give him a defense in his case against Lisle and Kerr.

For two years he devoted every moment he could to the study of constitutional law, while Jonathan Strong, his freedom in question, went fearfully about his work. Sharp's own lawyers, although they managed to have the case postponed, had no faith in his labors. Sharp persisted, however, and finally in an early edition of the authoritative Blackstone's *Commentaries*, he found an opinion quoted from an old case: "as soon as a Negro comes into England, he becomes free."

Much encouraged, Sharp hurried to consult the new (third) edition of the *Commentaries* which had just been published. To his dismay he found that the passage no longer appeared. The great Dr. Blackstone had been induced by the Chief Justice of the King's Bench, Lord Mansfield, to withdraw that opinion.

Still, Granville Sharp reasoned, the first edition was better than nothing. Besides, his reading had turned up other authorities who supported Blackstone's original view. He put the results of his researches into a long memorandum, which he submitted to Dr. Blackstone himself. To his relief the famous lawyer did not object to his arguments. Blackstone did, however, warn: "You'll find it uphill work in the Court of the King's Bench"—by which he meant Lord Mansfield.

Sharp's next problem was to convince his own lawyers. He arranged a consultation for them with the Solicitor-General and with Dr. Blackstone. At the consultation he learned that Dr. Blackstone did not wish to become involved in the situation and was now definitely against him. Sharp learned, also, that the Solicitor-General was eager to agree with Blackstone, and that his own lawyers did not dare open their mouths.

He admitted that it seemed useless to go on with the case when his own lawyers were against him, but before giving up, Sharp determined to make one more effort. This time he circulated, among twenty of the most eminent lawyers in Britain, manuscript copies of the memorandum that Blackstone had at first expressed no objection to. It appeared a hopeless attempt, even in Sharp's own view. But to his surprise and joy, it succeeded.

The twenty eminent lawyers recognized the memorandum as "a right reading of the law." This development so alarmed the lawyers of Kerr and Lisle that they withdrew their suit against Granville Sharp.

At long last Jonathan Strong was safe and presumably free, but Sharp was not satisfied. His purpose was not merely the freedom of Jonathan Strong; he wanted freedom for all the slaves in England, and he intended to force a definite decision from the courts.

This was not easy, for Lord Mansfield, the Chief Justice, although a kindly man and one of England's greatest judges, really did not want to render a decision on such a far-reaching issue. At the time, more than fourteen thousand slaves lived in England, and enormous sums of money were involved in this human "property." In Mansfield's opinion, if they were freed, the upheaval would be too dreadful to contemplate. He skillfully evaded the main issue in the instances of three slaves whom Sharp had rescued and whose cases he had managed to bring before the High Court. Each time, the Chief Justice ruled either that the owner could not prove his ownership of the "property," or he persuaded the owner to free the slave. In this way he avoided ruling on the legality of slavery itself.

In 1772, however, Sharp rescued a fourth Negro, named Somersett, and this time there was no clear way out for the Chief Justice. Somersett had been brought by his master from Virginia to England. He had escaped, had been recaptured by his master, and had been consigned on a ship for sale in Jamaica. It was from the ship that Sharp had rescued him.

Sharp worked harder than ever in the preparation of the case. He not only paid the preliminary expenses, but he provided Somersett's lawyer with a lengthy dissertation containing all the results of his own extensive legal researches.

At the trial Lord Mansfield tried his old tricks. He adjourned the case twice and hinted to the slave's owner that if he would set Somersett free, great difficulty would be avoided.

But the owner refused to release the slave, and Lord Mansfield was forced to concede that this time he could not avoid rendering a decision.

On a chilly June day he delivered his judgment with all the solemnity it deserved. "The state of slavery is of such a nature," declared England's Chief Justice, "that it is incapable of being introduced on any reasons, moral or political, but only by positive law. . . . It is so odious that nothing can be suffered to support it, but positive law. Whatever inconveniences, therefore, may follow from the decision, I cannot say this case is allowed or approved by the law of England; and therefore the black must be discharged."

In other words, since no *actual* law had established slavery in England, slavery could not legally exist there.

Granville Sharp had won. Almost alone and unaided, the mild little government clerk had cut the chains from England's fourteen thousand slaves, and secured the freedom of any slave who might be brought within her borders. Now one could truly say, along with the poet Cowper,

> *Slaves cannot breathe in England; if their lungs*
> *Receive our air, that moment they are free:*
> *They touch our country, and their shackles fall!*

It was a thrilling story. James Forten marveled at the power of one good man, even though he had neither money nor influential friends. He thought about how Anthony Benezet had inspired Granville Sharp, and he thought about the inspiration he himself was now receiving from Sharp. What would he do with that inspiration? James was not sure, but he knew it would have something to do with helping his own people.

James's working hours as a stevedore were long and hard, but at nineteen his strength seemed unlimited. He was seldom too tired to walk along the waterfront, when he had the time.

But, what he saw and heard there often filled him with despair.

It was 1785, thirteen years since Granville Sharp had brought about the abolition of slavery in England. Yet the English slaving ships still plied their ugly trade, and prospered. Liverpool was the greatest slaving port of all. Five-sixths of the evil traffic centered in this thriving city of some fifty thousand people. Almost every brick in its buildings, he was told, was "cemented with Negro blood." All classes of its people in some measure shared in the slave trade profits.

Most Liverpudlians, however, did not know this and were unaware of the conditions under which the slaves were bought, transported, and sold. They saw only the goods that they and their fellow countrymen had manufactured, which was put into the holds at Liverpool; and they saw the tropical produce with which the vessel returned. They usually did not know that after these ships had unloaded their British cargo at various ports, they then anchored on the West Coast of Africa. Here the ship's crew crammed the hold with shackled African victims whom they had either bought from other greedy Africans, or themselves had kidnapped from the native villages.

Liverpudlians, for the most part, were ignorant of the cruel Middle Passage during which many of the stolen Africans died from inhuman treatment. They heard little about the great profits the owners of the slave ships made when they sold their captives, either in the West Indies or in America. They were unconcerned that the shipowners made still another profit from their voyage, for once the Africans were sold, the ship holds were cleansed of their indescribable filth. Then the same holds were filled with sugar, rum, tobacco, and cotton, and the vessels returned to Liverpool to increase the prosperity of the fast-growing port.

But if the Liverpudlians were largely unaware of the cruelties of the slave trade, the seamen on these slave ships were not. Some of them told James what they had seen and heard. Their words filled him with an emotion he found hard to describe, even to himself. It was not hatred, because he was never able to hate. Sorrow, indignation, and despair were better words for his feelings. At any rate he felt he could not stay longer in Liverpool, where every ship he loaded or unloaded might be a detestable slaver.

But he was not yet ready to leave England. Perhaps, he told himself, London would be better. One foggy morning in late spring he took the stage and rode the two hundred tiring miles to England's greatest city.

In London, as in Liverpool, James had no trouble finding work on the waterfront. As before, when his day's work was done, he walked curiously about the city. Again he did not care for what he saw. The smoke and grime-blackened buildings, the dank, murky haze, the overcrowding of people and houses, the acrid, sulfurous air from the thousands of coal fires, all made him long for the fresh breezes, the open living space, and the bright sunshine of his American home.

He was astonished at the numbers of desperately poor people—ragged, half-starved looking. Everywhere were thin, pale little children who were forced to labor long hours at back-breaking jobs. He couldn't remember seeing such pitiful, driven-looking little creatures in Philadelphia, even though children there worked if the family was in need.

The drunkenness, especially among the working people, and the havoc it wrought, appalled him. He took a vow never to drink alcohol in any form, a vow he kept all his life. And the floggings. His eyes couldn't escape them. Servants, soldiers, sailors, vagrant paupers, school children—all were flogged for every offense for which no other easy remedy suggested itself.

This definitely was not the England of his dreams. Yet somewhere in the midst of this great, crowded city was Granville Sharp, and perhaps other, great-hearted men who thought as Sharp did. James resolved not to leave London until he had seen Sharp.

His opportunity came after he had been in London a

Granville Sharp

month. Although Sharp was not a Quaker, James reasoned that his activities on behalf of the slaves would keep him in contact with the Quakers who, in England as in America, opposed slavery.

One day, while strolling in Hyde Park, James saw a portly Quaker reading on a bench, and seated himself next to him.

As he had hoped, the Quaker looked at him with interest and began a conversation. The upshot was that the Quaker told James about a forthcoming public meeting on the slave trade which Granville Sharp was to address. Of course James would be welcome, the Quaker said.

The meeting turned out to be a poorly attended affair in a private house but, to the young stevedore from Philadelphia, it seemed the most impressive gathering possible, for seated on a stool at the side of the room was Granville Sharp.

James was not shy by nature, but he was overcome by the sight of the man he so admired and could not say a word. He gazed with awe at the fifty-year-old Sharp's slight, stooping figure, at the gentle face with its oversized nose and prominent chin, and at the bright, kindly gray eyes. Seated next to Sharp, James saw a big, broad-shouldered, rugged man about twenty-five-years old, named Thomas Clarkson.

Clarkson had recently won a prize at Cambridge University for an essay called "Is It Lawful to Make Slaves of Others Against Their Will?" Now he rose, and in a deep, slow voice told the meeting something about his essay. The information for it, he said, had come from the writings of Anthony Benezet. "And," he continued, "since I have learned of the shocking inhumanity of the slave trade, I have had little rest at night, often never closing my eyelids for grief." He paused and then announced to the gathering, "I have definitely concluded to devote my life to the abolition of the slave trade."

When Clarkson had finished speaking, he showed the audience a number of products from Africa—ivory, beeswax, palm oil, and woods used for dyeing. Then, while the group was exclaiming over these, he dramatically produced from a leather bag some fine-looking cloth, and articles of leather, gold, and iron.

"Look upon these," Clarkson urged. "They were made in Africa by native Africans. Do they not indeed represent a considerable degree of culture?"

James, who had never seriously thought about African civilization, was so moved by the sight of these objects that he longed to be away from these white men, to be alone to think about what he had seen and heard. He slipped out of the meeting into the drizzling London night.

This was the first of the antislavery discussions that young Forten attended in England. The voices of reform were few, but they were clear. Both Sharp and Clarkson spoke out continuously against the slave trade—at schools, universities, churches—anywhere they were permitted to speak. Clarkson, moreover, had won to the cause his friend William Wilberforce, a twenty-six-year-old member of Parliament from the Liverpool area. Wilberforce was sponsoring an Abolition Act in Parliament. In this he had the support of England's brilliant twenty-six-year-old Prime Minister, William Pitt. To these arguments, both in and out of Parliament, James listened with an avid ear.

Exactly when James Forten left England and returned to America is not known. But the fall of 1786 found him back in Philadelphia in a sail loft on Willing's Wharf, signing the papers that made him an apprentice to Robert Bridges, sailmaker.

6

The Black
Sea Captain
from Massachusetts

The early morning sun splashed so brightly through the window that James could barely see the outline of the mainsail he had chalked on the floor of the sail loft. He studied the drawing tacked to his workbench, which was the pattern for the large outline chalked on the floor.

The drawing on the workbench represented a real advance in James's skill as a sailmaker. He had constructed it himself from the measurements that Mr. Bridges had taken for a "suit of sails" for a new ship being built nearby. Soon he hoped to be able himself to take such measurements, for his employer had promised to teach him this art. Measuring for a suit of sails was a difficult task, involving skilled and complicated calculating. If the measurements were not correct, the drawings and the cutting to follow would not be accurate either. Then the sails would not fit the masts or behave properly in the wind.

James had come a long way in the past two years. His rise from apprentice to foreman in one of the largest sail lofts in Philadelphia was a record few twenty-two-year-olds could match. Of the forty sailmakers in the Bridges loft, half of whom were white and half Negro, only James could accurately cut sails all day without stopping, except at the noon hour. It was James, too, who most quickly grasped the principles of sail-making, and who could now take a sail from the drawing stage to the great canvasses, sewn and roped, ready to be *bent* (fastened) to the mast. No wonder that Mr. Bridges praised him for his "skill, energy, and good conduct."

Still there were times when the young foreman would rather stare idly out of the loft window than work. This was one of those days. He stood up and gazed down at the long line of wharves edging the river. Directly below him were the wharves and stores of Thomas Willing, whose immense shipping interests furnished sailmaker Bridges with much of his business.

As James watched, Willing himself came into view, stepping briskly among the sailors and the draymen, and nimbly avoiding the casks, bags, barrels, and boxes piled high on the docks.

He soon disappeared into one of his warehouses, and James's eyes returned to the river. To him, as to most Philadelphians, the Delaware was far more than a river. It was a broad avenue to and from the great world. From his window high in the sail loft he could see the stevedores loading the tall-masted merchant ships with the products of the energetic new nation. Often they sang as they rolled into the hold the barrels of salted beef, pork, and fish, apples, and onions, the tubs of butter and lard, the piles of wrought iron or bar iron, and here and there a bale of cotton.

James especially liked to watch the foreign ships coming up the river with cargoes of English woolens; wines, silks, and watches from France; and velvets from Spain. In the harbor now were ships that had brought mahogany from Santo Domingo, spices from the East Indies, sugar, oranges, lemons, and rum from the West Indies, and special rope from Russia for the sailmakers.

As the years passed, James observed in the harbor an increasing number of ships from far places and a more interesting variety of men of all nations and classes, characters and colors. One cloudy morning in the spring of 1793, the sailmaker, while doing an errand at the waterfront, noticed a ship

Looking up the Delaware River

anchored near the public landing at Pine Street. He stopped short and stared. There was nothing unusual about the ship. It was a smallish schooner named *Mary*, of Westport, and it smelled to high heaven of whale oil and bone, but on the deck he could see the captain and the crew. All were Negroes.

Before nightfall, James had managed to meet the captain, Paul Cuffe, a tall, broad, kindly looking man of thirty-four—half Negro and half Pequot Indian, and by religion a Quaker. The captain, just returned from a successful whaling trip to Newfoundland, had brought his cargo of whale oil and bone to sell in Philadelphia.

During the next few days the two men saw much of each other. Although the New Englander was modest and reticent, James was able to draw out part of his story.

Paul Cuffe was the seventh of ten children of a poor farmer who had been born in Africa and brought as a slave to Massachusetts. In time, Paul's father worked out his purchase price and bought his freedom. With his Indian wife, he moved to Cutterhunk Island, a lonely place nine miles from the mainland of Massachusetts. There he built a house, the only one on the island, and there all his children were born.

At thirteen Paul was barely able to read and write, but he kept at his studies, teaching himself, and occasionally getting help from some sympathetic white person on the mainland. Since he lived in a region that made its living mostly from the sea, he determined to learn the art of navigation. By swapping his labor for instruction, he managed to learn the rudiments of this skill, basic for a ship's officer.

In 1775, when he was sixteen, Paul became a common seaman on a whaling vessel bound for the Gulf of Mexico. His next trip took him to the West Indies. On his third voyage, made at the height of the American Revolution, he was captured by the British and imprisoned in New York—although not on the *Jersey*—for three months.

After his release, he went back to the family farm. With the idea of building and sailing his own boat, he devoted every spare minute to the study of arithmetic and navigation. When he was twenty, he and an older brother, David, built an open boat for trading with Connecticut people. On their first voyage, the brothers were set upon by local pirates, beaten, and their boat stolen. At this point, David decided to go back to farming, but Paul, undaunted, built another boat, by himself. This boat, like the first, was attacked by local pirates. They beat Paul, threw him overboard, and made off with his craft. He was lucky to get home.

He was determined, however, to have his own boat. Another was built, and for this he borrowed money, bought a cargo, and started for Nantucket. On the way, pirates again chased him, but he managed to escape. As he fled, he damaged his boat on a rock, and had to return to Westport. He repaired it, and finally reached Nantucket, where he sold his cargo.

His second voyage met with more misfortune. Other pirates robbed him of his cargo and left him, severely beaten, in the drifting boat. But since he still had his vessel, Cuffe felt that his situation was improving. With the third voyage, a good one, his luck changed. Soon he was making a nice profit from his ventures. He bought a new, covered boat of eighteen tons and sailed from his rented home on the Westport River for St. George—with a cargo of codfish. This voyage was the foundation of a profitable fishing industry near his home.

About this time Paul Cuffe married an Indian girl, Alice Pequit, and shortly afterward he engaged another Indian, his brother-in-law, Michael Wainer, to be his chief mate. In a new twenty-ton vessel, *Sunfish*, the two men made two successful fishing trips to the Strait of Belle Isle and Newfoundland. Cuffe used these profits to build the forty-two-ton schooner *Mary*, which lay now at the Philadelphia wharf.

Forten was particularly interested in Captain Cuffe's account of what had happened on the *Mary's* first voyage. The schooner, accompanied by two boats, and with a crew of ten—Negroes and Indians—had gone on a whaling expedition to the Strait of Belle Isle. When they reached the Strait, Cuffe found four other whaling ships already there, fully equipped with boats and harpoons.

The usual custom was for such ships to share the equipment, but these four New England captains grew angry and tried to drive the *Mary* away. Whether or not the four captains resented the schooner because its captain and most of its crew were Negro, Cuffe did not know. They told him it was because the *Mary's* crewmen were not experienced whalers, and the vessel did not have proper equipment. He preferred to believe them.

"Very well," he told his crew when he got the captains' message, "we'll go it alone."

Their activities alarmed the other whalers, who seemed

to fear that they would drive the whales away. When the Cuffe group caught its first whale, the other captains decided to share their equipment and to include the *Mary* in their whale hunts. Seven whales were taken, six of them by the crew of the *Mary*—two of these harpooned by Cuffe himself.

The whales had been particularly rich in oil and bone, Cuffe told James. With the proceeds from their sale in Philadelphia, he planned to buy the material for a larger ship he was building in his shipyard at his home near Westport.

The meeting of these two men, who were destined to become leaders of the American Negroes of their day, led to a lifelong friendship. In time, each was to advocate a radically different course of action for the Negro people to follow in their search for fair treatment and equality, but at their first association, both agreed upon one thing—they must "cultivate a love to all mankind."

7

A Shameful Incident—
and a Happy One

Despite his meeting with Paul Cuffe, James Forten looked upon the year 1793 as mostly a bad one. It was the year that Congress passed the first Fugitive Slave Act, which permitted a slaveholder, or his agent, without a warrant or the presence of a civil officer, to seize an alleged runaway slave and return him to his supposed master. In Pennsylvania, some decency remained, for if a Negro denied that he was the runaway slave in question, he was granted a hearing before a magistrate to prove his contention.

The year 1793 was also the time that the yellow fever gripped Philadelphia and killed more than five thousand of its fifty thousand inhabitants. How many Negroes perished of the deadly disease, James was not sure. He did know that many of the black people, under the leadership of Richard Allen and Absalom Jones, had risked their lives to nurse white victims and bury the dead at a time when few white persons were willing to carry on this necessary but dangerous work. Forten had joined in this valuable service. His strong arms gently lifted the pitiable victims and placed them in the cart that was to carry them to the emergency yellow fever hospital on Bush Hill.

When the plague was over, Mayor Clarkson and eminent doctors like Benjamin Rush publicly thanked the black people for their priceless help. Some Philadelphians, however, their gratitude fading as the danger diminished, attacked the Negroes. With few exceptions, this group declared, the Negroes had plundered the homes in which they had served and had shamefully neglected the patients.

One of the most prejudiced and venomous of this group was Mathew Carey, a printer and editor who had come from Ireland. Forten read Carey's "Short Account of the Malignant Fever Lately Prevalent in Philadelphia" with mounting anger and bewilderment. He was calmed down by Richard Allen and Absalom Jones. We can write and publish our side of the story, the two Negro leaders impressed upon him. This will give us a chance to say many things that are in our hearts.

Within a few months, Jones's and Allen's remarkable pamphlet "A Narrative of The Proceedings of the Black People during the Late Awful Calamity in Philadelphia in 1793" appeared. Forten, reading the pamphlet through twice, marvelled at the wisdom of these two ex-slaves, and at how effectively they defended the Negro people against slander.

In the back of the pamphlet were a few additional pages directed especially "To Those Who Keep Slaves, and Abhor the Practice." Forten read them with especial interest. Most slaveholders, Jones and Allen pointed out, do everything they can to keep the black people in a state of ignorance, and then criticize them for being ignorant.

"Yet," Richard Allen wrote, "we believe if you would try the experiment of taking a few black children and cultivating their minds with the same care, and let them have the same prospect in view, as to living in the world, as you would wish for your own children, you would find them upon the trial . . . not inferior in mental endowments. . . . If the black people seem inferior in their behavior, [perhaps it is because] the vile habits often acquired in a state of servitude, are not easily thrown off. . . . Why," inquired the two ministers, "will you look for grapes from thorns or figs from thistles? It is in our posterity enjoying the same privileges with your own, that you ought to look for better things."

Forten placed the thin pamphlet between the pages of the large Bible he read every night. Education, and a chance to use that education, is what the black people must fight for, he thought. Another thought stirred him: the power of the printed word could be used by black people as well as by white. If the printed word were to be effective, he realized, its message must be well thought out and well stated. James resolved to copy passages from the Bible and from Shakespeare's plays regularly so that he could improve his style of writing.

On a pleasant Sunday, in July, 1794, not long after Jones and Allen published their pamphlet, James Forten and his new bride (whose name is now unknown) attended the first service of the African Episcopal Church of St. Thomas, the first Negro church in the United States.

James was proud of the handsome brick building on Fifth Street, near Walnut, and he was moved by the words carved into its marble front: "The people that walked in darkness have seen a great light."

He was proud that the black people had been able to finance, plan, and construct such a fine church. They had done this although they were few in number, miserably low in income, and without the advantages of an education. True, they had had the help of a few white friends, Dr. Benjamin Rush and Robert Ralston among them. In the main, though, the church had grown from the seven years of self-sacrificing fundraising by the Free African Society, an organization of free Negroes founded by Jones and Allen to help members in time of sickness, unemployment, or other hardship.

The African Society had grown out of the shocking affair at St. George's Methodist Church. James Forten was not a member of St. George's, for he had been reared an Episcopalian. But like most Philadelphia Negroes, he often attended St. George's, especially when Richard Allen preached there. Although St. George's congregation was about sixty percent

African Episcopal Church of St. Thomas, 1793

white, its Negro members had helped build the church, both by contributing from their own pitiful funds and by donating their physical labor, no matter how tired they were from their own work.

In spite of this valuable contribution, the Negro members were made to feel more and more unwelcome. One morning, in November, 1787, their most respected members, Richard Allen and Absalom Jones, with a number of other Negro wor-

The Reverend Absalom Jones

shipers, were jerked from their knees during prayer and "or-dered out of the main part of the church and upstairs in the back where they belonged."

Shocked and grieved, the little group held a brief consulta-tion, and, as Allen wrote later, "all went out of the church in a body, and they were no more plagued with us in the church."

After the Negroes left St. George's, they began to work to establish a separate church to which only Africans and descend-ants of Africans could belong. Seven years of struggle produced not one Negro church, but two: the African Methodist Episco-pal Church whose pastor was Richard Allen, and the African Episcopal Church of St. Thomas, whose pastor was Absalom Jones. The Episcopal Church opened its doors twelve days earlier than the Methodist Church. Most of its members—formerly Methodists—proclaimed that they would never be

Methodists again after the way they had been treated at St. George's.

James Forten, who was elected to the first vestry of St. Thomas, observed within his lifetime the curious development of these two churches. The African Methodist Church, called Bethel, which held its first services in a small wooden building, formerly a blacksmith shop, separated itself completely from the white congregations. This church grew into a powerful organization among the Negro people, with great influence and many member churches throughout the nation.

The larger, and more well-to-do congregation of St. Thomas, which remained under the control of the white Pennsylvania Episcopal Diocese, continued as a fine individual church for Negro Episcopalians in Philadelphia. It never became a nationwide voice for the Negro people, as did the African Methodist Church, which was run by Negroes for Negroes. But Forten never regretted that his church remained within the white framework. He felt that by continued association—even a limited one—each group could give much to the other.

The snow swirled so quickly outside his sail loft window that James could scarcely see the river, which stretched dimly in the distance like a snow-covered meadow. James Forten was tired of winter in this year of 1798. For six weeks now, Philadelphia had lain frozen in the grip of one snowstorm after another. The Delaware was choked with ice, frozen so thick and hard in some places that loaded wagons were crossing on it from the New Jersey shore. Incoming ships could not come up to the wharves, and ships already in port were forced to stay there.

This inactivity on the river front did not harm the sail-making business. Ships that could not leave port took the opportunity to have new sails made and old ones repaired. At times James wished that business would slow down. Mr. Bridges was getting old, and was not very well. More and more

Thomas Willing

he let the management fall completely on his foreman's shoulders. James did not mind accepting this responsibility. After twelve years in the sailmaking business he felt he could run the whole loft if he had to. He wished, though, that he had more time to perfect a device he had invented, a device that made easier the management of large, heavy sails—always a problem on big ships.

One day when he was experimenting with a little model he had built of this sail-managing device, he looked up to find Thomas Willing watching him. Willing's shrewd eyes glinted with interest.

"What have you there, James?" he asked pleasantly.

Forten was glad to explain the invention. He had always

liked Thomas Willing. Ever since he could remember, the great shipowner, merchant, and banker had taken a kindly interest in him, had given him newspapers and books to read, and in general had encouraged him in his determination to become an educated man.

When James had finished his explanation, Willing gave him a friendly clap on the shoulder. "Remarkable," he said. "You are a remarkable man, James. But I must hurry along."

He disappeared into Bridges' office, and Forten got up to make sure that one of the apprentices was roping a sail properly. The snow was coming down harder than ever. Soon he would have to push through the drifts to get to his lonely home on Shippen Street.

His young wife had died soon after their marriage, and James had not yet found anyone else to fill her place in his heart. If he tired of reading, which he seldom did, or felt especially lonesome or hungry for a good meal, he could visit his mother and his sister Abigail, who lived close by in a house that he had bought for them. Ever since Abigail's husband, Dunbar, had been lost at sea, he had supported her and her two children, in addition to supporting his mother.

But, even with this companionship, the winter seemed unusually dreary. He was thankful when the snow melted, and Spring came with fresh vegetables and young lambs, shad and chickens to eat. Unfortunately, the coming of Spring did not make Mr. Bridges any livelier. Almost every day he told James that he would like to retire if he could find a good sailmaker and business man to take over the loft. He would, he said, like someone who knew his customers and knew all his forty employees, from the apprentices to the master sailmakers.

One afternoon about closing time, Bridges suddenly remarked, "You know, James, I'll never find a better sailmaker than you, or a better businessman either. How about you buying me out?"

"I, sir?" James felt a flush of pleasure, then a quick droop of spirits. Mr. Bridges' mind must be addled with age to think that he, a black man, could borrow so much money. That was one reason why there were so few Negroes in business. Bankers and businessmen generally did not believe that Negroes had the ability to run a business, and so they were not willing to lend them the money to get started on an enterprise.

But to his employer who waited for his answer, Forten said only, "I thank you for your compliment to me, sir, but you know I have no money to buy your business, as much as I would like to."

Bridges' eyes studied him rather sadly. "You're right, James. You have naught but your wages. A pity it is, too. Well, I suppose I'll have to start looking for someone to buy me out."

Bridges clumped wearily down the steps to the street, leaving behind him a worried foreman. Would the new owner want a black man as foreman, James pondered. The more he thought about the matter, the more concerned he grew.

If only he could borrow the money to buy the sail loft, he thought to himself, his problem would be solved. Suddenly he realized how quiet the loft was. It was long past quitting time. Everyone else had gone home. Forten locked up the loft and went out into the cold, early winter darkness.

In the Willing office below the loft, the candles still burned. James paused. This could mean that Mr. Willing was there. On impulse he opened the door and looked in. In a way he hardly expected to see the merchant-shipper there at this hour, but there he was, and alone, too. He was even looking at the young foreman in a friendly fashion. Some instinct, some inner voice urged James to take his problem to Mr. Willing, to ask him to lend him the money to buy Mr. Bridges' sail loft.

"And why not?" he asked himself as Willing consented to see him for a few minutes. After all, he believed he had the necessary training; he was sure he could run the business and repay the debt at the usual rate of interest as readily as could most sailmakers. The only way in which he differed from the other men asking Mr. Willing's aid in business matters was that his ancestors had been stolen and brought over here from Africa.

Thomas Willing listened carefully to James Forten's request. He asked him many questions about how he planned to continue the business. After awhile he told the young foreman that he would discuss the matter with Mr. Bridges, consider it from every angle, and let him know as soon as he could.

A week later Willing summoned Forten to his wharf office and agreed to lend him the money to buy Robert Bridges' sail loft. In return, Forten promised to outfit all Willing's ships with the device he had invented to make the handling of sails easier.

Thus it was that one of the shrewdest businessmen in the new nation demonstrated his faith in the ability of the bright, hard-working young Negro he had known from childhood.

James Forten took over the Bridges sail loft sometime during the summer of 1798. In his own place as foreman he appointed Charles Anthony, a competent Negro sailmaker who remained his "good right arm" for thirty-seven years. Of his entire work force of thirty-eight men, only one of the nineteen white employees left, saying that he preferred to work for a white employer.

8

"Seven Hundred Thousand Enemies"

In 1800, the capital of the United States was to be moved from Philadelphia to Washington, but this coming event appeared to make small difference in the booming, zooming activity of the Pennsylvania city. It was still the largest city in the new nation, with slightly over 74,000 white people and nearly 7,000 Negroes, 85 of whom were slaves, and the rest free.

The waterfront especially was a hustling, bustling place, noisy with the rumble of carts on cobblestones, echoing with the shouts and songs of the stevedores, and gay with the flags and streamers of hundreds of tall ships rocking at the wharves. Most of the ships made regular voyages between Philadelphia and the European ports. Others engaged in the China and East Indian trade or sailed frequently to the West Indies.

It was one of these West Indian vessels which, on a chilly morning in August, 1800, attracted James Forten's attention. Yesterday the ship's captain had approached him about making a new suit of sails for the vessel. Now, as James went on board to take the measurements, his flesh suddenly went cold. Something about the ship, perhaps a subtle odor he remembered from his experience in England, perhaps the half-hidden squares of African cloth he had noticed in the captain's cabin, made him feel that the vessel was engaged in the slave trade. Abruptly he faced the captain.

Philadelphia waterfront in 1800

"What, sir, may I ask, was your cargo aboard ship last voyage?"

The captain looked surprised. "Why, Jamaican rum."

"And what cargo to Jamaica—perhaps from Africa?" James's usually pleasant face looked tight and angry.

The captain hesitated before answering, just long enough to make Forten feel he had guessed the truth. "Good day to you, sir," he said, courteous in spite of an inner wrath, "were I starving, I would not make a sail for a slaver."

He let himself over the ship's side into his small dory and rowed back to the dock, his face hot with anger. He was still angry when he climbed the stairs to his loft, but soon the calm, clean atmosphere quieted him. He looked at his hard-

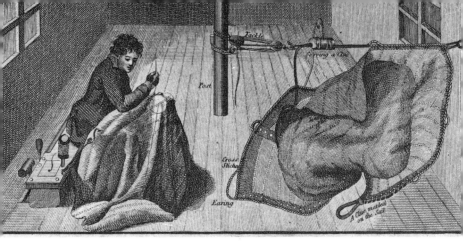

Worker in a sail loft, 1794

at-work apprentices and journeymen with affection. He would vouch for the character of each one, for he supervised his employees with care. Although sail lofts, as a whole, were characterized by heavy drinking and profane language, Forten did not permit these activities in his establishment.

His sail loft, which he had now owned for two years, was one of the most prosperous of the eighty-odd lofts in Philadelphia. Its success was due partly to James's invention of the sail-handling device, and partly to his reputation for "neat and durable work and strict integrity in all his dealings." Business was so good that he could afford a fine, three-story brick house on Lombard Street to which he took his new wife, Charlotte, a slim, lively girl with glossy, dark-brown curls.

At the age of thirty-four, Forten the sailmaker was well aware of the "blessings and enjoyments" of his own life. He was also aware of the wretched existence that many, perhaps most, of the people of his color endured in the United States. Indeed, their situation was worse than it had been in 1789, when the United States became a nation.

The invention of the cotton gin was largely responsible for this. It had made the growing of cotton immensely profitable. Unfortunately, cotton growing was easier and profits were larger with slave labor than with non-slave labor. Thus on the Southern cotton plantations the demand for slaves grew. With the demand came the traders, eager to make money by buying and selling human beings.

This greed knew no limits. As soon as Congress passed the first Fugitive Slave Act, in 1793, greedy men, from the North as well as the South, watched for any Negro who might be an escaped slave and so could be returned to his master with hope of reward. They not only hunted escaped slaves. They often kidnapped free Negroes and sent them South to a "master" who was glad to claim them.

By January of 1800, this evil had become so widespread and so unbearable that "the Free Blacks of Philadelphia" petitioned Congress for aid in fighting it. "We are happy and grateful to live in freedom under the American form of government," they told Congress, "but we cannot ignore the hardships under which many of our people must labor."

In the petitioners' opinion, all the people of color had equal rights under the Constitution with other Americans; but now the Constitution itself was being violated as persons from some Southern states were kidnapping Negroes in Maryland and Virginia, transporting them to Georgia, and inhumanly selling them, an act "degrading to the dignified nature of man."

"By these and other measures injurious to the human species," the free Negroes wrote, "there are 700,000 Blacks in slavery in these states. Relieve the hard condition of our race," they prayed Congress, "revise the Fugitive Slave Act and the laws relating to the slave trade, and adopt such measures as shall *in due course* emancipate our brethren from the present situation."

James Forten was among the first to sign the petition. His neat signature stood out boldly among the scrawls and X's of petitioners who could not write their names. The petition itself was handed to Representative Robert Waln of Pennsylvania, a Quaker Federalist. He presented it to Congress and moved that it be referred to an appropriate committee.

Immediately the battle was on. Representative John Rutledge of South Carolina jumped up, white with rage, and shouted:

> Lay the petition on the table. Already too much of this new-fangled French philosophy of liberty and equality has found its way and is too apparent among these black "gentlemen" in the Southern States, by which nothing will do but their liberty.... They now tell the House these people are in slavery. I thank God they are; if they were not, dreadful would be the consequences.... Further they say they [fugitive slaves] are sent to the Southern states. Who can prevent that? Persons possessing slaves can send them there if they please.... I consider this subject very improper and unconstitutional to discuss, and from the ill-effects it might produce, we should say no more on it.... I hope it will never be called up hereafter.

"I can see no good reason why the petition should not be committed," Congressman Waln answered mildly. "Every petition presented to the House ought to receive that attention. To reject the present petition without an examination can have no good effect."

Next, Representative Smilie, a hardheaded farmer-lawyer from Western Pennsylvania, took the floor, declaring:

> Much of this petition *is* within the power of the House. In so far as the House has the power, I consider it the duty of this body to attend and grant relief. We must consider [these people] part of the human species equally capable of suffering and enjoying with others,

and equally the objects of attention. Therefore they have a claim to be heard.

The condescending voice of Representative Harrison Otis of Massachusetts, from the Federalist side of the House, answered him:

I hope that this petition will not be committed, for I have never seen a petition presented under a more dangerous and unpleasant aspect. It appears to be subscribed by a number of individuals who are incapable of writing their names, or of reading the petition, and all the more certainly of digesting the principles of it....

To encourage a measure of this kind must be mischievous to America very soon. It will teach them the art of assembling together, debating, and the like, and would soon, if encouraged, extend from one end of the Union to the other. Although I thank God I have no slaves, nor ever wished to possess any, I think I had better leave the regulation of it to those who are cursed with it. If any grievances exist, they are properly and only the objects of legislation in the several states, not of the General [Federal] Government.

Representative Henry Lee of Virginia jumped to his feet to agree. He remarked:

I observe that the gentlemen were sent to the House to protect the rights of people and the rights of property. That property which the people of the Southern States possess consists of slaves, and therefore Congress has no authority but to protect it, and not take measures to deprive citizens of it.... I hope the House will never intermeddle with the property of any of its citizens. I wish to return the petition to the gentleman who presented it.

As Lee sat down, Rutledge, the South Carolinian, demanded to be heard. Even to consider this subject is improper, he told his colleagues. Indeed some of the states never would have come into the Union if they had not been promised that Congress would never legislate on slavery.

Amidst a slight stir, Representative George Thacher of Massachusetts asked for and gained recognition. His voice came clearly and calmly. "Would any gentleman say that it was a policy not to legislate about 700,000 enemies in the very body of the United States?"

He paused and looked around at the angry and distressed congressmen. "*While they are slaves,*" he said, pounding out each word, "*they are enemies.* A greater evil than the very principle could not exist; it is a cancer of immense magnitude that will some day destroy the body politic, except a proper legislation shall prevent the evil. It must come before the House sooner or later. Then why postpone it?"

In a quieter tone, Thacher continued:

> I contend that the petition, which is couched in as decent and respectful terms as is possible, should be referred. Whether the petitioners are black or white, whether they can write, or whether not, is entirely immaterial; they state their suffering is under a law of the United States, and that is enough for a respectable reference. Because they cannot write, are not their rights to be secured to them? Strange doctrine. A great reason why they cannot write is their being brought up in early life in slavery.

Thacher took his seat amid a strange silence. A fellow New Englander, John Brown, a wealthy shipowner of Rhode Island, arose, and said:

> I do not hold a slave in the world, but I am as much for supporting the rights and property of those who do as

though I were a slave owner. I consider this as much personal property as a farm or a ship.... I do not fear the power of 700,000 enemies that the gentleman has pointed out, since there are five million to withstand them. They can at any time subdue them.

... The country needs money. It needs a navy. We ought therefore use means to obtain it. We ought to go further and repeal the slave bill all together, for why should we see Great Britain getting all the slave trade to themselves? Why should not our country be enriched by that lucrative traffic?

I beg the gentleman who put the petition up to take it back again.

Through the murmur that greeted this statement came the voices of the congressmen from Delaware and Maryland, who denied that their citizens were involved in kidnappings. "Indeed," boomed Christie of Maryland, "the Fugitive Law is not strong enough. I suggest people be fined not only for harboring a black, knowing that he or she is a slave, but also if they know the black is not a slave. Throw the petition under the table," he added contemptuously.

He was supported by Jones of Georgia who shouted in a tone of outrage:

... The petitioners contemplate that these people [the slaves] ought to be represented with us and with the rest of the citizens of the United States. They speak of themselves as "We, the people of the United States of America." They speak of the Federal Compact [the Constitution] as representing them in common with others....

I would ask the gentlemen here whether with all their philanthropy they would wish to see these people sitting by their sides deliberating in the councils of the nation. I presume not. These people go farther and say, "We do not ask for the immediate emancipation of all, but we ask you to prepare the way for the oppressed to go free, that every yoke might be broken, thus keeping up the principle to do unto others as you would they should do unto you!"

... I believe it might have been happy for the United States if these people had never been introduced amongst us ... [but they are here and are the property of individuals. Since the Constitution guarantees the rights of property] ... how then can this House meddle with that part of our property? The General Government has no power over it.

Congressman Waln, a worried look on his face, said, "If I had known that this petition would have caused so much alarm, I certainly should have desired the petitioners not to present it. But," he emphasized, "if they had still thought it necessary and been desirous of it, I should have presented it. I deem it my duty whenever any individual conceives himself injured by a law, to receive his petition."

On and on the arguments went. One of the last to speak that day, William Edmond of Connecticut, said:

I am as far from wishing to affect the property of citizens as any gentleman. Much less should I wish to affect the Constitution. But this appears to me to be a very respectful petition.

It matters not whether the people are black or white. Only the petition is to be regarded, and not the color of the persons who, representing their grievances, ask for such relief as the Constitution can afford them. Surely every measure ought to be adopted to alleviate their sufferings. ... Is contempt the way to recommend attachment to the government?

Mr. Rutledge of South Carolina did not like the way things were going. He moved that the House adjourn, and it did.

When the House of Representatives met the next day, there was a subtle change in the attitude of most of the congressmen. Representative Thacher could feel it as he took the floor and with a slightly humorous twist of his mouth said:

> For the sake of argument, I am willing to admit that slavery does exist and that it is sanctioned by the laws and Constitution of the United States. I do not believe this, but as some other gentlemen do, I will admit it for the present. Surely, would it not be desirable that this great evil should be destroyed if it can be done without injury, nay, with advantage to its possessors? Does the petition go any further than this? It does not.

Thacher looked around, but only a hostile silence greeted him. Even Congressman Waln had turned his head.

Late that afternoon a resolution was presented in answer to Waln's proposal that the "Petition of The Free Blacks of Philadelphia" be sent to a committee and considered. "That the parts of the said petition," stated the resolution, "which invite Congress to legislate upon subjects from which the General Government is precluded by the Constitution have a tendency to create disquiet and jealousy, and ought therefore to receive no encouragement or countenance from this House."

"Vote. Vote on the Resolution," called several voices.

The vote was quickly taken. Eighty-five congressmen voted "yea"—that such petitions do "create disquiet and jealousy and should not be encouraged." Only one congressman —Thacher of Massachusetts—cast a "no" vote. Eighty-five to one, the House of Representatives voted not even to listen to the voice of the free Negroes, crying out for justice, and to be treated as men.

The Philadelphia Negroes soon learned what had happened to their petition. Most of them were downcast and shocked at the enmity displayed by many of the congressmen

2.1134

toward their people. One group, including Forten, met at the St. Thomas Church to discuss the matter. James's glance went to some of the brave, familiar faces. Stout-hearted Absalom Jones sat silent, unhappy-looking. Cyrus Bustill, the prominent baker who had supplied bread to the Revolutionary Army, absently tossed and retossed into the air the silver piece that George Washington had given him as a souvenir. Even Richard Allen appeared too weary of spirit to plan anything new.

But Forten the sailmaker did not give in to discouragement. "At least we have one steadfast friend in Congress—Representative Thacher," he told the group. "While one voice speaks for justice, there will be those who hear."

He left the meeting early to write a letter to Thacher. James thoughtfully and slowly built the letter as he wrote:

> We, . . . sir, Africans and descendants of that unhappy race, thank you for the philanthropic zeal with which you defended our cause when it was brought before the General Government, by which we can only expect to be relieved from our deplorable state. . . .
>
> Though our faces are black, yet we are men, and though many amongst us cannot write because our rulers have thought proper to keep us in ignorance, yet we have the feelings and passions of men and are as anxious to enjoy the birth-right of the human race as those who [use our ignorance as an argument against our petition]. . . .
>
> While some, sir, consider us as much property as a house or a ship, and would seem to insinuate that it is as lawful to hew down the one as it is to dismantle the other, you, sir, more humane, consider us a part of the human race, and . . . would say that our thralldom is unjust.
>
> Judge what must be our feelings to find ourselves treated as a species of property, and levelled with the brute creation; and think how anxious we must be to raise ourselves from this degrading state.

Unprejudiced persons, who read the documents in our possession, will acknowledge that we are miserable. Humane people will wish our situation alleviated. Just people will attempt the task, and powerful people ought to carry it into execution. Seven hundred thousand of the human race were concerned in our petition. Their thanks, their gratitude to you they now express. Their prayers for you will mount to Heaven, for God knows they are wretched, and He will hear their supplications.

A deep gloom now envelops us, but we derive some comfort from the thought that we are not quite destitute of friends, that there is one who will use his endeavors to free the slave from captivity, at least render his state more sufferable, and preserve the free black in the full enjoyment of his rights. . . .

As James signed his name to the letter he decided to pass a resolution for himself—to do everything in his power to change the unsympathetic attitude of his fellow-countrymen toward the Negro people.

In the late summer of 1800, however, an incident occurred that made many of Forten's fellow-countrymen even less sympathetic than they had been before. In the State of Virginia, Gabriel Prosser, a twenty-four-year-old Negro slave, planned an extensive revolt in which several thousand slaves were to kill their masters and as many white people as they could. Then they were to march on Richmond, seize the arms stored in the Capitol there, and demand the freedom of all the slaves in the state.

Whether or not the revolt would have succeeded will never be known. On the eve of the planned uprising, a violent storm interfered with operations, and two slaves, who could not bear to see their kind masters killed, revealed the plot to the authorities. The white population reacted with a surge of fear and distrust of the Negro. All at once the "700,000 enemies in the very body of the United States" that Representative Thacher had spoken of became uncomfortably real to many people who had never before taken such a possibility seriously.

Forten the sailmaker heard of Prosser's revolt, and of two smaller and equally unsuccessful slave revolts, with dismay. His people, he believed, were on a wrong and dangerous road. Violence could and would bring nothing but violence in return. And as Congressmen Brown had pointed out, why should the white people fear the power of 700,000 "enemies" when there were five million whites to withstand them? Violence would not liberate; it would only further enslave. The road to liberation lay through education and training, through slow and involved legal processes. The road was long and mostly uphill, but it was, he thought, the only way to a real and lasting freedom for his people. There was no other.

9

Letters
by a Man
of Color

In the gray, early-morning cold of January, 1807, Forten the sailmaker stood awhile on the wharf near his sail loft and gazed out over the Delaware River, as he always did before going to work. Ice had come into the water during the night, and he watched a small boat maneuver through the ice chunks toward the dock. Suddenly from somewhere close to where he stood came a splash and a scream. Before his horrified eyes a man's pale face, gurgling and gasping, appeared in the icy river.

Forten threw off his heavy cloak, plunged into the freezing water, and grasped the drowning man by his hair just as he began to sink out of sight. A few minutes later Forten had made his way back to the dock, swimming with one arm and keeping the gasping victim afloat with the other. On the dock James wrapped his cloak around the shivering man and carried him up to the warm sail loft where he lay on a pile of canvas until he regained his strength.

This man was not the first nor the last person that Forten rescued from drowning in the river. In 1821, when he was fifty-five-years-old, Forten made a rescue that attracted the attention of the Humane Society of Philadelphia. They presented him with a certificate on which the following inscription appeared:

> The Managers of the Humane Society of Philadelphia, entertaining a grateful sense of the benevolent and

Top portion of Humane Society certificate awarded to Forten

successful exertions of James Forten in rescuing, at the
imminent hazard of his life, four persons from drowning
in the river Delaware at different times, to wit: one on
the—day of the 11th month, 1805; a second on the—day
of the 1st month, 1807; a third on the—day of the 4th
month, 1810; and on the—day of the 4th month, 1821
present this Honorary Certificate as a testimony of their
approbation on his meritorious conduct.—By order of the
Managers, Joseph Crukeshank, President, Philadelphia,
Fifth Month, 9th, 1821.

Actually Forten, a powerful swimmer since boyhood, had, according to Lydia Maria Child and other prominent anti-slavery workers who knew him, saved as many as twelve persons from drowning. He had kept no record of his rescues, however, and the Humane Society was able to credit him with only four.

If James Forten was admired by the white people of Philadelphia as a saver of drowning persons, the black people of the city loved him for another kind of rescue work. He rescued numbers of them from slavery by giving them the money to buy their freedom. Perhaps the best known of the slaves whose freedom Forten secured were the father, mother, three sisters, and two brothers of the Reverend John Gloucester who, in 1807, founded the first African Presbyterian Church in the nation.

On a rainy night in March of that year the Reverend Gloucester met in a schoolroom with James Forten, Richard Allen, Absalom Jones, and other leading Philadelphia Negroes. Their purpose was to prepare a resolution thanking God that Congress had passed an act prohibiting the importation of slaves into the United States after January 1, 1808.

The business part of their meeting finished, the talk of the men turned to Paul Cuffe. They were all proud of the black Quaker sea captain from Westport, and heard of his success with real pleasure. Cuffe, who had begun his career with a small rowboat he had built himself, was now the owner, or part-owner, of several vessels which had sailed around the world. Just a year before, in 1806, he had sailed to Russia, Sweden, and Denmark in his fine new ship of 268 tons, the *Alpha*.

Now James Forten had news for the group. "I've had word," he told them with a tinge of excitement, "that Paul will be here soon. He's bringing a number of passengers from Helsingör, Denmark to Philadelphia."

But it was September before Captain Cuffe and the *Alpha* anchored in the Delaware. As soon as Cuffe discharged his passengers and unloaded his cargo, he hurried to Forten's sail loft. The captain was not alone. With him was a husky, blond youth who smiled at James in a friendly way, but said nothing.

"This is Abraham Rodin, my apprentice," Cuffe explained. "He signed on with me at Gothenburg. He hasn't learned to speak English yet, but he will soon."

Forten was interested in the young Swede who had asked the kindly Cuffe to take him to America and teach him the art of navigation. He devoted particular attention to the "Indenture of Apprenticeship" that Rodin had signed in which he bound himself to Paul Cuffe as an apprentice for six years, beginning June 22, 1807.

Captain Cuffe, anxious to get back to his family in Westport, stayed only a few days in Philadelphia. Before he left, he mentioned to James a subject that he said was very close to his heart, something that he called "the redemption of Africa," which was to aid the black people in America as well as in Africa.

It was well that Cuffe's ship *Alpha* reached Westport before President Jefferson's Embargo Act of December, 1807, went into effect. This Act was a desperate attempt to protect American shipping from depredations by both the British and the French, who were at war with each other. Each nation maintained that the United States was helping the other by transporting supplies, and so was fair game for attack. England was particularly offensive because she persisted in taking American seamen off American ships and impressing them into the British Navy, which needed men.

Under the Embargo, American ships could not bring cargoes to American ports from Europe or carry cargoes out of American ports. In this way Jefferson hoped they would avoid trouble. Unfortunately, instead of protecting American commerce, the Embargo seriously hurt it. Soon the entire business outlook of the young nation darkened. In Philadelphia James observed grass growing on some of the wharves, and ships rotting at their moorings.

One morning he watched a large group of resentful, hungry, and penniless sailors, a few Negroes among them, waving the Stars and Stripes, march to the City Hall and beg the Mayor for help. But the Mayor could give them none.

"You constitute an unlawful assembly," he told them. "Lower your flag and disband at once."

The sailors did as they were ordered, but despair was on their faces as they broke up into small, angry groups, trying to decide what they could do next. The following day a number of private citizens, including James Forten, contributed money for their care until other work could be found for them.

Fourteen months after Jefferson's Administration had enacted the Embargo, it admitted the Act was a failure, and repealed it. Other measures designed to help the young nation weather the economic storms caused by Napoleon's insane ambitions in Europe were hurriedly passed. These, too, did little to improve conditions in American seaports, and American ships everywhere continued in danger.

Forten was somewhat uneasy therefore in June, 1810, when he received word from Paul Cuffe that in London he had been given such encouragement by The African Institution concerning his idea for "the redemption of Africa" that he planned to visit that continent in the fall. He was going to Sierra Leone, a colony on the west coast of Africa managed by the London African Institution, as the humanitarians Clarkson, Wilberforce, and Sharp called their organization. If, in Cuffe's observation, Sierra Leone seemed to be a suitable place for "sober families of black people in America to settle among the Africans," he intended to convey them there in his own vessel.

The Quaker sea captain was not able to complete his plans by the fall of 1810. But on New Year's Day, 1811, Paul Cuffe, in his new ship *Traveller*, sailed out of Philadelphia for Sierra Leone. Nine Negroes composed his crew. Who else went with him or what cargo he carried on this voyage is unknown.

Nor is there a known record of what James Forten did on the winter's day that the *Traveller* left on its perilous voyage to a mysterious land. But there is little doubt that his prayers and good wishes for the captain, crew, and passengers must have gone with the ship as it stood out in a strong wind for Delaware Bay.

By April, 1811, James received word that the *Traveller* had safely reached Sierra Leone. He was greatly relieved, because conditions on the high seas were even worse now for American ships than they had been in 1807. In fact each passing week seemed to bring increasing reports of American ships plundered by the British and robbed of their seamen, who were then forced into the British Navy.

On June 19, 1812, President Madison declared war on England. He had been goaded into this action partly by England's high-handed actions on the seas and partly by the demands of Henry Clay and other War Hawks from the Western Frontier. On the Eastern seaboard, the war was unpopular. Merchants and shippers despaired as business approached the vanishing point.

In Philadelphia, as elsewhere, unemployment was high. The available work simply would not stretch to include large numbers of Negroes, mostly without training or skills, who began to flock into the Pennsylvania city.

This influx of unskilled black people from other parts of the country was watched with dismay by the Philadelphia Negroes, who on the whole were the best educated, the wealthiest, and perhaps the most highly regarded people of African descent in the nation. Nevertheless, they could understand why the others came, and they sympathized.

Pennsylvania, a free state since 1780, lay on the border of the slave states. It had a reputation for treating all its people humanely. Early in its history, humanitarians like Benezet, Franklin, and Dr. Rush worked not only for the abolition of slavery but also for the education and training of free Negroes. In Philadelphia Negroes had a chance to rise to positions of respect in the community, and many did. If they became sick or destitute they were not turned away from the public hospitals and poorhouses. It was no wonder that Negroes who had recently been freed, or were free but oppressed, or those who simply had run away from their masters, headed straight for the Quaker city.

But in a community of slightly over 75,000 people, this "alien" group stood out with shocking visibility. Consequently, trouble soon arose. One observer of the situation described it this way:

> Freed from the shackles but not from the vices of slavery, these victims of inhumanity throng our streets in search of pleasure or employment. Some indeed embrace the opportunities ... of obtaining honest support. But ... [the] refugees show a tendency to huddle together in cities and large towns. They depress the wages of Negroes already there, and by causing surplus unskilled labor give rise to crowds of loitering, mischievous beggars, a nuisance to the community.... No state in the union has been more exposed to incursions of black inhabitants from others than Pennsylvania. Accordingly they are daily flowing in upon her—occupying the time of her criminal courts—filling her jails and poorhouses, and sauntering through her towns and villages in misery and want.

By February, 1813, a number of white Pennsylvanians found the situation so intolerable that they petitioned the State Legislature for "relief." The petitioners "prayed" that:

          1. a law be passed requiring all Negroes to register with the state;

          2. any Negro coming into Pennsylvania be registered within 24 hours or face fine, imprisonment, and possible sale;

          3. authority be given to sell for a term of years the services of those Negroes convicted of crimes;

          4. a special tax be levied on the free Negroes for the support of their poor.

Forten read this petition with concern. It had already passed the lower house of the Pennsylvania Legislature, and was now before the Senate. But surely, he told himself, the intelligent, fair-minded white people of the state would not want such a law passed. The trouble was that so few of them were aware of this proposed act. What should be done?

All night he sat in front of his parlor fireplace and pondered the problem. Toward dawn, as the black spruce logs shot out showers of sparks, he decided to try himself to make the people of Pennsylvania aware of the evils of this proposed law. He stayed home from the sail loft and began to write. Sheet after sheet of paper fell to the floor, as James wrote on.

He was shaken by the sickening possibility that some legislators did not look upon the Negroes as men. "Why are we not to be considered as men?" he asked.

> Has the God who made the white man and the black left any record declaring us a different species? Are we not sustained by the same power, supported by the same food, hurt by the same wounds, wounded by the same wrongs, pleased with the same delights, and propagated by the same means? *And should we not then enjoy the same liberty, and be protected by the same laws?*

The original framers of the Pennsylvania Constitution did not intend to exclude Negroes from the benefits of the document, James pointed out. When they declared that all men were born equally free and independent, "they did not particularize white and black because they never supposed it would be made a question *whether we were men or not.*"

Forten was especially distressed by the section of the bill which permitted police officers to arrest

> ... any black, whether vagrant or man of character, who cannot produce a certificate of registration. He is to be arrayed before a justice who is thereupon to commit him to prison!
>
> The jailor is to advertise a *Freeman*, and at the expiration of six months, if no owner appear for this degraded black, he is to be *exposed to sale*, and if not sold, to be confined at hard labor for seven years!
>
> The constable, whose antipathy generally against the black is very great, will take every opportunity of hurting his feelings! ... Perhaps he sees him at a distance, and having a mind to raise the boys in hue and cry against him, exclaims, "Hallo! Stop the Negro."
>
> The boys, delighting in the sport, immediately begin to hunt him, and immediately from a hundred tongues is heard the cry, "Ho, Negro. Where is your certificate!"
>
> Can anything be done more shocking to the principles of civil liberty! ....
>
> My God, what a situation is his! Search the legends of tyranny and find no precedent ... It stands alone.

As to the Registration section itself, which stated that a black man must be registered within twenty-four hours after his arrival in the state or be liable to a fine, to arrest, imprisonment, and sale, the sailmaker asked:

> Who is this Register? A man, and exercising an office where 10 dollars is the fee for each delinquent, will probably be a cruel man and find delinquents where they really do not exist.
>
> The poor black is left to the merciless gripe [grasp] of an avaricious Register; without an appeal, in the event

> of his tyranny or oppression. O miserable race, born to the same hopes, created with the same feeling, and destined for the same goal, you are reduced by your fellow creatures below the brute.

For a few minutes after he had written the last sentence, James sat, too emotionally upset to go on. Then he took up his quill and began again to write:

> ... There are men among us of reputation and property, as good citizens as any men can be, and who pay as heavy taxes as any citizens are compelled to pay; and still even they are not exempted from this degrading bill.
>
> The villainous part of the community, of all colors we wish to see punished.... Enact laws to punish them severely, but do not let them operate against the innocent as well as the guilty.... Punish the guilty man of color to the utmost limit of the laws, but sell him not to slavery. If he is too indolent to labor for his own subsistence, compel him to do so; but sell him not to slavery.
>
> Many of our ancestors were brought here more than 100 years ago; many of our fathers, many of ourselves, have fought and bled for the independence of our country. Do not expose us to sale. Let not the spirit of the father behold the son robbed of that liberty which he died to establish, but let the motto of our legislature be, "The law knows no distinction...."

Suddenly, James felt unaccountably weary. "I have done," he wrote. "My feelings are acute...."

He thrust his quill into the little sand pot on his desk. There was no time to waste. If his writings were to aid his people, they must be read by the voters of Pennsylvania, especially by members of the State Legislature. He could not spend valuable hours hunting for someone to share the cost of getting his arguments before the people. With his own money, and mostly by his own efforts, James Forten published and distributed his writings in a small pamphlet called "A Series of Letters by A Man of Color."

The logic and emotional appeal of Forten's *Letters* had a powerful effect. The proposed law was defeated. Nearly a quarter of a century was to pass before other legislation, so humiliating and dangerous to the Negroes and so damaging to the American concept of freedom as the Registration Bill of 1813, was introduced into the lawmaking body of Pennsylvania.

10

Black Pioneers

Although the odious Registration Bill was defeated, the situation of the Negroes in Pennsylvania did not improve. One reason for this was that the war continued to go badly for the Americans.

From his sail loft window James could see the British ships cruising brazenly on the Delaware. In the streets he heard the blare of bugles and the beat of drums as the government tried to arouse an interest in the war. Sometimes, on the outskirts of the city, troops of the feeble little American Army fought sham battles and invited the public to watch them. But very few young men volunteered to fight. The fire of patriotism appeared to blaze mostly in the American Navy.

On September 10, 1813, Captain Oliver H. Perry, against great odds, swept the enemy from Lake Erie. Eleven nights later, when Philadelphia glowed with thousands of lights in honor of this victory, Forten the sailmaker joyfully placed a burning candle in each window of his home. Perry's victory was doubly sweet to him. It was an American victory, and Negro seamen had played an important role in the triumph.

It was common knowledge that at first Captain Perry had not been pleased to have Negroes in the crew of his squadron on Lake Erie. When Commodore Chauncey sent what Perry called "a motley set—blacks, soldiers, and boys," the young captain complained. His complaint brought a swift reply from Chauncey:

> I regret that you are not pleased with the men sent
> you ... for to my knowledge a part of them are not sur-
> passed by any seamen we have in the fleet: And I have yet
> to learn that the color of the skin, or the cut and trim-
> mings of the coat, can affect a man's qualifications and
> usefulness. I have nearly fifty blacks on board of this ship,
> and many of them are among my best men.

Probably even while he complained, Perry realized there
was no point in his doing so. In a war that few people supported, Negroes already formed from 10 to 20% of all American naval crews, and the navy knew it was lucky to get them.
Without these black sailors, the United States vessels would
have been even more dangerously undermanned than they
were. Shortly after the famous battle on Lake Erie, Perry
praised the Negroes in his crew. "They seemed," he said, "absolutely insensible to danger."

The American victories on the Great Lakes did not, as
many people hoped, bring the war to a quick end. As the year
1814 dawned, the American situation grew rapidly worse. For
some Philadelphians the first realization of this came at dusk
on a February night when a strange, unpleasant odor floated
through the city. The officials were trying to burn tallow and
old fat in the street lamps because they could no longer bring
in whale oil through the British blockade. The old fat did
not give a satisfactory light. The citizens cursed the darkness
as they stumbled through what once had been the best-lit
streets in America.

But by August 25, dim streets and bad smells became un-
important. A clear and present danger was at hand. On this
date, couriers, riding to the city in hot haste, spread frightening
rumors and swift alarm. Washington, the capital city, the
Capitol itself—the proud symbol of the new nation—had fallen,
burned by its arrogant conquerors.

Even at the moment, cried the couriers, the British General Ross, the destroyer of the Federal City, was advancing on

Baltimore. If Baltimore fell, surely Philadelphia would be next. Citizens must act swiftly to prevent disaster.

At ten o'clock the next morning, thousands of Philadelphians assembled in Independence Square. Many were clearly fighting panic. Merchants, shipowners, clergymen, lawyers, physicians, and bankers joined with carpenters, bricklayers, stone masons, and other artisans in demanding immediate measures to protect the city. Ex-Governor McKean, an elderly hero of the Revolution, presided at the meeting.

The old man raised a confident hand, and the excited babble quieted. Before noon, McKean told the crowd, there would be a Committee of Defense, made up of Philadelphia's most able men. The Committee would see to it that fortifications were erected to defend the city. The people were to go home and await orders.

The Committee, meeting in haste, quickly determined where the fortifications were to be. Next it asked who would build them. The answer came instantly. "Everybody." Everybody? Did that mean the banker and the shipowner? The minister? The shoemaker? The ditch digger? It did. Everyone who had the strength was to give one day of hard labor to the defense of the city. Then someone asked, "Shall we include the black people?"

There was a brief pause, then a discussion among the members of the Committee who agreed that the black people should definitely be asked to join in the city's defense. "Well, how much labor can they be expected to contribute?" one member inquired. "Let us leave it to their leaders," was the decision, "to James Forten, Richard Allen, and Absalom Jones."

No one of the men—Forten, Jones, or Allen—wasted time or words when the Committee of Defense approached them. Within two days they enlisted twenty-five hundred Negroes, each of whom agreed to give not one, but two days of labor to the cause. Forty-eight-year-old James Forten, with twenty journeymen from his sail loft, led the Negro group as they marched the long hot miles from Independence Square to Gray's Ferry, west of the city. Here, for forty-eight hours, they dug and piled up earth until the earthworks construction was complete.

Fortunately for Philadelphia the British did not reach the city. They were stopped outside of Baltimore, and their superior force of warships was defeated by a tiny, gallantly fighting American fleet on Lake Erie. But still the Americans could not be sure the war was over, and their army desperately needed men. James Forten, remembering the Negroes who had fought bravely in the Revolution, set about raising a "Black Brigade."

On a bitter-cold day in February, 1815, this brigade marched across the ice on the Delaware River to Camden to join other American troops in the area. Then the news came. The war—the second war for American Independence—was over. The service of the Negro volunteers was not needed.

The Peace Treaty had actually been signed weeks before, on Christmas Eve, in Ghent, Belgium. But because news traveled slowly, in January, 1815, the Americans fought and defeated the British in a fierce, unnecessary battle at New Orleans.

Many free Negroes had fought with Andrew Jackson's troops that day. When the battle was over Jackson made a Proclamation to them in French, the language of the free blacks of the area.

James Forten read a translation of that Proclamation about the time he heard that peace was restored in the land.

> Soldiers. When on the banks of the Mobile, I called you to take up arms, inviting you to partake of the perils and glory of your white fellow-citizens, *I expected much from you;* for I was not ignorant that you possessed qualities most formidable to an invading enemy. I knew with

what fortitude you could endure hunger and thirst, and all the fatigues of a campaign.

I knew well how you loved your Native country, and that you had, as well as ourselves, to defend what man holds most dear—his parents, relations, wife, children, and property. YOU HAVE DONE MORE THAN I EXPECTED. In addition to the previous qualities I before knew you to possess, I found, moreover, among you a *noble* enthusiasm which leads to the performance of great things.

Soldiers! The President of the United States shall hear how praiseworthy was your conduct in the hour of danger, and the Representatives of the American people will, I doubt not, give you the praise your exploits entitle you to. . . .

A few days later, on February 15, 1815, Forten wrote a letter to Paul Cuffe, who had returned from Sierra Leone to his home in Westport.

Dear Friend,

It has pleased the Almighty disposer of all things to once more bless this late distracted country with Peace, which to you and all Christians must be welcome news indeed. It is out of the power of man to describe the greater joy that was manifested by all classes of Society in this city. Indeed the people for some time appeared to be most frantic.

His pen moved more slowly and thoughtfully as he wrote:

I approve very highly of your proposition of building a ship for the African trade by the men of color . . . and shall lay it before the Society [Philadelphia African Institution] when we meet and write you their opinions. . . .

Charlotte and the Family join me in love to your family. . . .

I remain very affectionately yours, James Forten.

PAUL

CAPTAIN

CUFFEE

1812.

Captain Paul Cuffe

This idea of Cuffe's of establishing a colony of American Negroes in Africa and providing for the prosperity of that colony by developing trade between it and the mother country was one that Forten now considered often. In the eight years since Paul had first broached the subject, James had with great interest watched the Quaker captain undertake ventures to bring his dream closer to reality.

Yet Forten could not go all the way with Cuffe on the subject of resettlement in Africa, for there were important differences in the background and experiences of the two men.

Paul Cuffe, the son of a slave stolen from Africa, was positive that the plan was a good one, and would work. As a child he had listened to his father's memories of that continent. Africa, his father had told him, was a place where men had wives and children and homes and villages and work to do, as did men everywhere.

As a man, Cuffe the sea captain had sailed to Africa in his own ship, a vessel he had built himself, with the help of other Negroes. He had lived in Africa and observed its suitability as a new homeland for American Negroes who wished to settle there. He had made friends of the Africans and of the African chiefs. From these he had won assurance that they would welcome and sell, or assign, land to any Negro settlers who wished to come into their territory.

The United States, Paul Cuffe believed, was a land of *white pioneers*, of men who had left their own homelands to seek a better life for themselves and their children in a new, wild, and relatively unsettled country.

Why, Cuffe reasoned, should not Africa become a land of *black pioneers* who were returning to the land of their ancestors, which was also a new, wild, and relatively unsettled country, to make a better life for themselves and their children. In doing so, they could take to the native Africans the knowledge and skills the black people had learned in America.

To James Forten, African resettlement was a "sometime yes" and "sometime no" thing. He, too, was a man of wide experience, wider than that of most Americans of his day. He also had lived in Europe and observed the ways of other nations. As Philadelphia's leading sailmaker, he knew and talked to men from many climes and from all walks of life. But it was hard for him to feel connected in any real way with Africa. His ancestors had been Pennsylvanians for generations, and he felt himself to be absolutely and completely American. When he tried to visualize what Africa was like, his mind's eye saw only the jungles, the wild beasts, the disease-making climate, and the half-savage men that most white Americans believed made up the whole of the "Dark Continent."

Yet he believed that there was much sense and much hope for the American black people in Captain Cuffe's plans. He believed this sufficiently to agree to become head of the Philadelphia African Institution, a branch of the London African Institution, which was fostering a colony of former British Negroes in Sierra Leone.

Forten had shared in Cuffe's disappointment when in March, 1814, the House of Representatives, by a vote of 72 to 65, rejected the measure, already passed by the Senate, that would have authorized President Madison to permit Cuffe to leave the United States with a vessel, emigrants, and cargo for Africa. Congress had refused Cuffe's request because any vessel sailing to Sierra Leone, a British colony, required a British license. The British, Congress suspected, would grant such a license only if they thought that in some way it would help them in their war with the United States.

But Paul Cuffe would not give up his dream. He went quietly ahead with his plans so that, when the war was over, he would be ready to carry them out. By December of 1815, his preparations were complete. He picked up a small group of emigrants and necessary supplies at Philadelphia, and around the first of the month sailed out toward Delaware Bay. James Forten, watching on the dock until the brig dropped from view, offered a prayer for the safety of Captain Cuffe, the *Traveller*, its 'Negro crew, and the black emigrants who were sailing bravely to the land of their ancestors to make a home for themselves and their families.

The emigrants were rich in courage and hope, but poor in worldly goods. When, on December 10, the *Traveller* picked up the final group of pioneers at New Bedford and sailed for Sierra Leone, thirty-eight emigrants were on board. Only eight of these were able to pay their expenses. For the other thirty, Paul Cuffe himself paid all costs.

All through the cold winter and unusually chilly spring Forten wondered whether the *Traveller* had made it across the treacherous ocean to Sierra Leone. Then on May 29, 1816, a letter came to him from Freetown, the capital of the colony:

> Esteemed Friend,
>
> I am happy to have the privilege of announcing to thee my safe arrival after a passage of fifty-four days. I was favored to land all the passengers at Sierra Leone, all in good health. The Governor has granted them lands to farm, all who wished to have land....

Eager to learn more of the American settlers, Forten was disappointed to read only a list of business matters in Philadelphia that Cuffe wished him to take care of. His next writing would tell more of the colonists, Cuffe promised, as he ended his letter, "My love and good wishes to thee and thy family and all inquiring friends."

This letter was the last untroubled communication between the two friends, for the Cuffe settlement at Sierra Leone unwittingly set in motion a train of events that soon brought great distress to James Forten and thousands of free American Negroes.

11

The American Colonization Society– The Great Debate

The summer of 1816 was a strange one, if indeed it could be called a summer at all. Night after night, even during July and August, frost glistened on the window panes of James Forten's fine home on Lombard Street. The tall brick house echoed with the happy, shrill voices and the running feet of lively children, for James and Charlotte had eight in all, although the birth dates of each are not now known.

Their firstborn was Margaretta, and then came Sarah, Harriet, James Jr., Robert Bridges, Mary Isabella, Thomas Willing, and William Deas. They were all bright, healthy, and talented. The wealthy, fifty-year-old sailmaker felt reasonably sure that all would grow up to happy, useful lives in the land where their ancestors had lived for generations—America.

But in December Forten's pleasant outlook for his family changed; for down in Washington, D.C. a group of men met to discuss the problem of the "free people of color" in the United States. Most of these men honestly wished to help the free Negroes whom they felt were doomed by increasing racial prejudice, and by the handicaps this prejudice brought about, to a life of poverty and humiliation.

Some of the men at the meeting, however, were not sincere in their expressed wish to help the free Negro. In their hearts they wanted primarily to protect the slaveholder. To them the presence of the free Negroes threatened the institution of slavery itself. They feared that numbers of educated, successful, free Negroes would prove that black men were not inferior beings. If they were not inferior, there was no justification for holding them in slavery. In addition, these men believed that the presence of free Negroes inspired the slaves to escape, or even to revolt against their masters. "The free people of colour," some openly declared, "are a dangerous and useless part of the community."

The irony of the situation was that both groups, each with a different motive, agreed upon the same solution—an organization "to promote and execute a plan for colonizing (with their consent) the Free People of Colour residing in our country, in Africa, or such other place as Congress shall deem most expedient."

On New Year's Day, 1817, this organization, the American Colonization Society, was formally established. Judge Bushrod Washington, the nephew of George Washington, was elected President, and Henry Clay one of its vice-presidents. Its Board of Managers included Andrew Jackson, Francis Scott Key, and ten other prominent men. Some of the ten were slaveholders, but others such as Robert Ralston, Richard Rush, son of Dr. Benjamin Rush, and the Reverend Robert Finley had been convinced by Captain Paul Cuffe that the greatest fulfillment for the American Negro lay in a return to the land of his ancestors where he could establish a nation of black men ruled by black men.

The humanitarians in the group believed that once the fear of the free Negro was removed, slaveholders would emancipate their slaves more readily. Freeing a slave was often a difficult matter, hedged about by prohibitive conditions. Many slaveholders who would have liked to be free of the burden of slavery—for it was often a burden—hesitated to turn their slaves out into a hostile community, unprepared as they were to live in a free society.

If, the humanitarians reasoned, these newly freed slaves

had a country of their own to go to, freeing them would be far easier. In this view they were supported by James Monroe, newly elected President of the United States, who, during his entire term of office, actively cooperated with the Colonization Society.

News of the formation of the American Colonization Society bewildered and shocked James Forten. For years—since 1807 in fact—he had been proud to know that a Negro, Paul Cuffe, could dream of being a nation-builder. Not only to dream, but to plan and carry out the establishment of what might become a modern nation.

But now a chill of apprehension crept through him. Somehow the existence of an actual Colonization Society, composed entirely of white men, with a definite territory in Africa under their control, brought into the situation a new factor.

Was Paul Cuffe's splendid dream to be used by unfriendly persons to drive the free black people from the land of their birth? To deport them to Africa? Cuffe had never envisioned colonization as deportation. Nor was Forten convinced that the slaves would be freed to go to Africa. Who among the Colonizationists had *proposed* that the slaves be freed to be sent away? No one, not openly at any rate. Only the free people of color were mentioned.

Round and round went James Forten's thoughts in a whirl of confusion. If only he could talk to Paul Cuffe. But Paul was sick, very sick, although in his New Year's message he had made no mention of his illness. Once again James read Paul's words, sent from his home at Westport, Massachusetts:

> Dear James, thou art often the companion of my mind.... Give my love to the members of the African Institution and tell them I wish them a joyful New Year, hoping they have all their energies renewedly engaged to celebrate the year in behalf of the African race and to the honour and glory of God....

On January 25, 1817, James Forten wrote a letter to Paul Cuffe. It was a letter he wished he did not have to write, but he felt he must answer the message [now lost] that Paul had sent to him shortly after the New Year letter. James wrote:

> Esteemed friend,
> ... the African Institution met at the Rev. Richard Allen's the very night your letter came to hand.... I must now mention to you that the whole continent seems to be agitated concerning the colonizing of the People of Colour.... Indeed the People of Colour here was very much frightened at first. They were afrade that all the free people would be compelled to go, particularly in the Southern States.
> We had a large meeting of males at the Rev. Richard Allen's Church the other evening. Three thousand at least attended, and there was not one sole that was in favour of going to Africa. They think the slaveholders want to get rid of them so as to make their property more secure. However, it appears to me that if the Father of all mercies is in this interesting subject (for it appears that they all think that something must and aut to be done but do not know where nor how to begin) the way will be made straight and clear.
> We [presumably the African Institution] however have agreed to remain silent, as the people here, both white and colored are desired against the measure. My opinion is that they [the Negroes] will never become a people until they come out from amongst the white people, but the majority is disidedly against me as I am determined to remain silent, except when they ask my opinion which I freely give when asked....

James could not bring himself to describe to Paul exactly what had happened at that meeting at Bethel Church, when over 3,000 frightened, almost hysterical free people of color had jammed into the small structure all looking to him, to Richard Allen, and to Absalom Jones, their leaders, for help.

The Reverend Richard Allen

It had not been the time, Forten had sensed, in any way to plead the cause of the Colonizationists. In their excited state, no one would have listened.

Besides, he himself was not sure just what the Colonizationists planned to do. They spoke with two mouths, and, he feared, perhaps neither mouth spoke the words that Paul Cuffe would have spoken. All James wanted was to help his people lead lives of usefulness, contentment, dignity, and honor. He was willing to explore any path that might lead to this goal for them, whether the path led to Africa or to continuing struggle and heartbreak at home.

This is what he had had in mind when he agreed to serve as Chairman of the meeting. But at that agitated gathering there had been no exploration of the Colonization Society's motives—whether good or evil. There had been only a desperate agreement that the free people of color must "remonstrate against the contemplated measure, that is to exile us from the land of our nativity." Out of this agreement had come several resolutions, which James had read in his clear, pleasant voice:

> Whereas our ancestors (not of choice) were the first successful cultivators of the wilds of America, we, their descendants, feel ourselves entitled to participate in the blessings of her luxuriant soil, which their blood and sweat manured; and that any measure or system of measures, having a tendency to banish us from her bosom, would not only be cruel, but in direct violation of those principles which have been the boast of this republic.
>
> We are resolved. 1. That we view with deep abhorrence the unmerited stigma attempted to be cast upon the reputation of the free people of color that "they are a dangerous and useless part of the community" when in the state of disenfranchisement in which they live, in the hour of danger they ceased to remember their wrongs, and rallied around the standard of their country.
>
> 2. That we will never separate ourselves voluntarily from the slave population in this country; they are our brethren by the ties of consanguinity, of suffering, and of wrong; and we feel there is more virtue in suffering privations with them, than fancied advantages for a season.

Perhaps Forten hesitated a moment before reading the third resolution. Seemingly it revealed a lack of belief in the capacity of the Negro people to be a pioneering and self-governing group. In their discussions neither he nor Paul Cuffe had exhibited this lack of faith. But the two ministers, Jones and Allen, had especially asked for this resolution, and so he read it:

> 3. Resolved, that without arts, without science, without a proper knowledge of government, to cast into the savage wilds of Africa the free people of color, seems to

us the circuitous route through which they must return to perpetual bondage.

The fourth resolution declared that "having the strongest confidence in the justice of God, and philanthropy of the free states, we cheerfully submit our destinies to the guidance of Him who suffers not a sparrow to fall, without his special providence."

This meeting in Bethel Church had no effect upon the American Colonization Society. Its officials proceeded with plans to acquire territory in Africa suitable for colonization by American Negroes. This was no easy matter, for the soil had to be rich, the water good, the Africans friendly and willing to sell the land. In addition, Society officials wanted to be sure that there would be no conflict with European nations which had already taken part of Africa for themselves.

To the members of the Colonization Society, as to most people in Europe and America, Africa was truly the "Dark Continent." No one of them had ever been there, nor in truth had the slightest desire to go. Yet, the members realized, some one must look over the land and choose a site. But who would volunteer for such a strange and dangerous task?

While they pondered, a thirty-four-year-old minister, Samuel Mills, from Connecticut, came to them in Washington and offered to go to Africa and find a suitable tract of land for the American Negro colony. Mills, who is credited with being the first American Missionary to foreign lands, knew Paul Cuffe. Months before he had talked to the Quaker sea captain and become convinced that Cuffe's idea of a return to the land of their ancestors was the best solution for the problems of the Negroes in America. Now, after he had won the Colonization Society's approval for his African journey, Mills wrote Cuffe, seeking information about the region near Sierra Leone which Cuffe had selected for the settlers he had transported to Africa in 1815.

Cuffe was grateful that Mills and the Colonization Society were going ahead with what he hoped was his own plan for the American Negro people. He was now too ill to do more than lie on his bed and dictate an occasional letter.

On July 9, 1817, he wrote to James Forten. Unfortunately this letter, penned over 150 years ago, has been lost, but Forten's reply, written on July 25, 1817, remains.

> Dear and Esteemed friend,
>
> This will inform you that your favor of the 7th month 9 came safe to hand, and I am extremely sorry to find by it that you have been dangerously ill.... I am very happy to inform you that we have at present in our City an African Prince, the grandson of King Surker from the Coste about 50 leagues to the south of Sierra Leone. He is about eight years of age, sent from the Coste to Havana and from there to the Abolition Society for his education. He is now in charge of Robert Douglas, he was ten days at my house, I am in hopes that his education here may be of benefitial servis to the cause. It may have the tendency of opening a correspondence between King Surker and the Society which may result in something advantageous to the community, and that the Almighty may make him the instrument of doing great good.
>
> The African Institution is very much concerned about the will of Mr. Samuel Gisle [who had freed his slaves] but they do not know what they can do with them, the slaves at present, but I hope and pray that the time is not far distant when there will be an asuylum for those poor soles to take their rest....
>
> I will thank you should you receive any information from the African Institution of London to please apprise us of the same should you think it proper.... Charlotte joins me in love to your wife and all the Family. I remain very affectionately yours,   JAMES FORTEN.

About the time Paul Cuffe was reading this letter from

Forten—a letter which showed that the sailmaker was still considering the founding by American Negroes of a nation in Africa, another communication went out from Philadelphia. This letter was, in one way or another, to affect the lives of millions of Americans yet unborn.

It was written by the Reverend Mills to Ebeneezer Burgess, a professor at the University of Vermont. Mills wanted Burgess to go with him to the west coast of Africa to select a suitable site for colonization by American Negroes. Since Burgess, like Mills, was a humane man, the young minister emphasized that their activities would in part consist of obtaining information about the slave trade which would induce the American government to suppress this illegal traffic. They would have the spiritual, if not the actual aid of Paul Cuffe. Mills wrote, in part:

> Paul Cuffe has been requested by some of the citizens of Sierra Leone to commence the colony at Sherbro. He only wants the aid of our government to do this. Paul wrote me last January that it was his opinion that more than half of the people of color in Boston and vicinity would embrace the first opportunity to go out to Africa.
>
> My brother, can we engage in a nobler effort? We go to make freemen of slaves. We go to lay the foundation of a free and independent empire on the coast of poor, degraded Africa. It is confidently believed by many of our best and wisest men that if the plan proposed succeeds, it will ultimately be the means of exterminating slavery in our country. It will eventually redeem and emancipate a million and a half of wretched men. It will transfer to the coast of Africa the blessings of religion and civilization, and Ethiopia will soon stretch out her hands unto God.

Perhaps if James Forten could have read the Reverend

Portrait believed to be of James Forten,
by an amateur Philadelphia artist

Mills's letter to Burgess, and Burgess's acceptance of what both men genuinely considered a "noble mission," he would have felt easier in his heart about the activities of the Colonization Society. Perhaps it would have made no difference. At any rate, the fears of the free Negroes grew and grew. In Philadelphia and in New York, where they were the most prosperous and most respected, this feeling that they were all about to be deported rose to the panic level and stayed there.

Naturally their feelings and wishes influenced Forten.

Certainly he, the wealthy owner of the largest sail loft in Philadelphia, a business he had built by his own industry and talent, had more to lose than most American Negroes if he were forced to leave his native land.

The Colonization Society did, of course, state that the African colony was to be for American Negroes *who would go there with their own consent.* Yet James Forten knew enough about human nature to fear that once such a colony existed, the temptation to send all free Negroes there would be tremendous. In the North as well as in the South, the power of the slaveholding interests was great. In Congress they wielded more power than their numbers warranted. It would be possible, Forten feared, for the slaveholders to persuade Congress that the best interests of the nation would be served by deporting *all* free Negroes to Africa. Once Congress agreed to this, it might pass a law making such deportation compulsory.

Would Congress actually pass such a law? Who could promise definitely that it would not, James Forten thought unhappily. It was evident to him that the voices of idealism which had spoken so strongly in the days of the Declaration of Independence were dying down. If the sad truth be told, the black man's place on the scale of human dignity in America was going down, not up.

Near the end of July the American Colonization Society announced plans for an Auxiliary Colonization Society in Philadelphia. Reacting with alarm, thousands of free Negroes crowded into the schoolhouse at Green's Court on the night of August 10, 1817. At this meeting, as at the first anti-colonization gathering, Forten was asked to serve as chairman. Tall, imposing in build, straight as a mast, he stood before his people and gazed around at the anxious faces sweating in the August heat.

When the room was completely quiet, he began to read "An Address to The Humane and Benevolent Inhabitants of the City and County of Philadelphia," a statement he and the other Negro leaders had put together some days earlier.

The Free Negroes, declared the *Address*, wanted no part of colonization—it would bring them not benefits but great harm. In this they spoke not only for themselves, but for the slaves, who had no voice. A colony where the freed slaves could be sent represented a constant danger both to the newly freed Negro and to the slaves left behind. The newly freed slave sent to the colony, and because of slavery unaccustomed to fending for himself, would soon fall victim to the perils and vices of Africa. Of the slaves left behind, the ones who showed courage and spirit in standing up for the rights that God had given to all men would soon be sent to the colony, while the tame, submissive slaves would be kept and subjected to increased hardships since none would dare protest their wrongs.

Since [the Negroes feared] it would be the slaveholder who decided which slave would be freed and sent to the colony:

> Parents will be torn from their children—husbands from their wives—brothers from brothers—and all the heartrending agonies which were endured by our fore-fathers when they were dragged into bondage from Africa, will be again renewed, and with increased anguish. The shores of America will, like the sands of Africa, be watered by the tears of those who will be left behind. Those who shall be carried away will roam childless, widowed, and alone over the burning plains of Guinea.

James heard a few sobs in the room, but he went on with his reading:

> Here in Philadelphia, where the voice of the suffer-ing sons of Africa was first heard, where was first commenced the work of abolition ... let not a purpose be assisted which will stay the cause of the entire abolition

of slavery in the United States, and which may defeat it altogether ... and which must insure to the multitudes whose prayers can only reach you through us, MISERY, sufferings, and perpetual slavery.

The long reading was finished. Forten called for a vote on whether the *Address* should be accepted. "Yea, yea," shouted the throng, a ring of hope in their voices.

Printed copies of the *Address* were distributed throughout Pennsylvania and sent to the Pennsylvania members of Congress, but this effort did not bring the result the Negro leaders had hoped for. Shortly thereafter, the Philadelphia Colonization Society was established as a branch of the American Colonization Society. Its leaders came to Forten and offered him one of the highest posts in the government of the proposed colony.

"You will," they said, "become the Lord Mansfield of this Heaven-born republic on the western coast of Africa."

James Forten stared sadly at the faces of his visitors. They were, he saw, good men who meant well.

"Thank you," he answered in a mild tone and with his usual courtesy, because he doubted that these good men realized what they were saying, "but I would rather remain as James Forten, sailmaker in Philadelphia, than enjoy the highest office in the gift of your Society."

The Colonizationists left, and Forten sat quietly in his parlor, alone with his thoughts. He knew that he had spoken truthfully to the Colonizationists, and the knowledge that he had done so comforted him. For the first time in many weeks he felt a lifting of his spirits. It was not in his nature to be deceitful. Yet he realized that he had not been entirely open in revealing his feelings about the Colonization Society. Even as he had walked to the Green's Court schoolhouse to read the *Address*, he had not been sure in his mind about the Colonization Society. This conflict, he felt sure, stemmed from a dream for his people that he shared with Paul Cuffe.

None of the other Negro leaders had his problem. They had not been to England and seen with their own eyes the humane faces of Sharp, Clarkson, and Wilberforce who from the first had encouraged Cuffe in his colonizing venture. No one of the other leaders had been so close to Paul as he.

While Paul Cuffe was in touch with him, he could believe with Paul in the goodness that motivated at least some of the men in the Society. He could share the faith that Paul, the brave, adventurous one, had in the pioneering qualities of the Negro people themselves. He could agree with Paul that Africa, a great, naturally rich continent, offered many possibilities for the development of a modern Negro nation within its vast borders. But now Paul's persuasive voice, too weak to speak even to his family, was stilled. If he had any advice to give James about the Colonization Society, he could not.

As the summer darkness fell across his garden, James Forten further searched his soul. Could he have acted otherwise? The other Negro leaders had no doubt that colonization was wicked and destructive to the Negro people. The entire free Negro population, it seemed, agreed to a man with these leaders. Should he have spoken against their wishes, especially when he was not certain of his own? In all honesty, he did not see how he could have behaved differently, James concluded, as he got up to light the lamp near the window.

Early in September, 1817, Captain Paul Cuffe died. And before another year had gone, thirty-five-year-old Samuel J. Mills, on his way home from Africa, died aboard ship of a fever he had picked up on that continent.

Mills had not been able to acquire the territory he had wanted. The African chiefs, who had promised the land to Paul Cuffe, went back on their word. Mills had, however, made arrangements for another tract of land, Sherbro Island, fifty miles south of Sierra Leone. The climate was not so healthful nor was it in any way so desirable as the territory for which Cuffe had negotiated, but it was the best the inexperienced young minister could do. This land was the beginning of what was first the colony of, and later, in 1847, became the Republic of Liberia—the land of the liberated.

Paul Cuffe dead. Samuel Mills dead. James had loved and respected Paul Cuffe, and he had respected what he knew of Mills; but now that they were gone, the conflict in his mind dissolved completely. Not only did he lose all interest in promoting an American Negro colony in Africa; he dedicated himself to an all-out battle with the Colonization Society.

12

Streams
of Hate

On New Year's Day, 1820, Forten the sailmaker, like men
everywhere, wondered what the coming year would bring. At
fifty-four years of age he knew his blessings, and he was thankful for them. He was thankful he had never been sick a day
in his life. He was thankful for his intelligent, good-looking,
healthy wife, and their eight fine children. He was grateful for
the prosperity of his business. And he was thankful for his
many, many friends, both black and white.

His white friends were mostly shipowners, sea captains,
and well-to-do merchants. Often to the stare of many, Forten
strolled arm in arm about the docks with these prominent
persons, speaking chiefly of business matters. With none of
these men, not even with Thomas Willing, who was now
eighty-nine years old, did he discuss the worry that was growing in his heart. This worry was that, as 1820 began, the Negro
people had far fewer white friends in the United States than
they had had thirty years earlier, when the nation was new.

But with his Negro friends he behaved differently. These
friends were of all kinds, for the rich and privileged sailmaker
never cut himself off from the humble majority of his people.
To them he revealed the thoughts that burned in his mind.
He found they shared his feelings. They, too, were aware that
white friends of the Negro people were vanishing fast.

All the Philadelphia Negroes were, for example, aware
of the "fire incident." Fire, an ever-present danger to all city

homes, attacked the Negro sections of Philadelphia with even greater fierceness than it did the white sections. In bitter winter weather the occupants of these flimsy hovels frequently crowded their fireplaces with roaring fires to fight the icy winds that blew in through the cracks in roof and walls. Often flames raced up the crumbling chimneys and set fire to the roofs. But although the Negroes shouted "fire, fire" and ran with leather buckets to the water pump, usually no fire company responded to their cries.

This was not surprising. At the time firemen were not employed by the city to fight all fires, but by private subscribers who paid a fee to have their own homes protected. Frequently the firemen stood idly by while a nonsubscriber's home burned to the ground. Whether Negroes could—even if they had the money—engage these private companies is not certain today. In any case the Philadelphia Negroes, feeling that they had no protection against fire, decided to form their own fire-fighting company.

Immediately, shouts of protest went up all over the city. All fire groups except for two Quaker companies angrily demanded that "this great danger to Philadelphia" be stamped out at once. So violent was the opposition to the Negro firefighters that young colored men trying to raise money for the project were attacked in the street.

Heartsick, James Forten watched this turmoil. Something had to be done quickly to stop this strange, rising tide of ill will.

Forten served as chairman of a hastily called meeting of "leading persons of color." He had no liking for what he felt he had to say. "We must abandon our plan for the African fire-fighters," he told the perplexed gathering. "Else [unless] the agitation is stopped, further trouble will ensue to our race."

The Negroes looked at each other in bewilderment. What harm could it do to have a Negro fire company in the

Negro area? Why should they not rely upon themselves if they could not rely on the white fire companies? No one of them could give a satisfying answer.

As the months went by, the bewilderment of these frightened and discouraged free Negroes increased, for all about them they could feel the hatred growing. Some said it was like the waters of four rushing streams which had merged into one mighty deluge of hate.

One stream arose from the angry discussions in Congress that preceded the passage of the Missouri Compromise of 1820. These debates about whether Missouri should enter the Union as a free or as a slave state were so bitter and so violent that when old Thomas Jefferson heard of them, he cried out that they were "like a firebell in the night, tolling the knell of the Union." Their ugly words still swirled about the nation, creating a hostile feeling toward all Negroes.

A second stream gushed from the flow of poor Irish and German immigrants who, about 1815, began to come to this country in ever-increasing numbers. In the Northern cities they competed with the free Negro for unskilled or semiskilled jobs. At first, there seemed to be jobs for all, but in 1819 there had been a depression, and work was hard to find. Soon the untrained immigrants and the free Negroes were rivals for even jobs such as ditch digging, chimney sweeping, and street cleaning. Enmity flared between them. The Negro was at a disadvantage in this struggle. When work was scarce, the white employer almost always gave the job to the white worker, even though he might be an immigrant just off a ship.

One morning after a heavy snowstorm, Forten, fighting his way through huge drifts to his sail loft, noticed with some bitterness that while "thousands of persons were employed in cleaning the gutters, levelling and removing the drifts, among the whole number there was not a man of color to be seen, when hundreds of them were going about the streets with shovels in their hands, looking for work and finding none."

The current of the third stream of hate washed first over the slave and then backwashed over the free Negro. Its source lay in the invention of the cotton gin, in 1793, which made the raising of cotton, especially with slave labor, immensely profitable. In 1794, before the gin was in common use, only 4,000 bales of cotton were produced in the United States. In 1820 cotton production rose to over 256,000 bales. To satisfy the demands of the cotton planters, even though the Constitution prohibited bringing in African slaves after 1808, the slave trade continued illegally. More and more slaves were "bred," and the net of slavery was drawn tighter around the unfortunate people already caught within its meshes.

As the number of slaves increased on a plantation, the white owners and their families had less personal contact with them. When the master did not know the slave as a person, it was easier to regard him, not as a man, but as "working property" like a horse or an ox.

In this way the presence of the free Negroes—who were undeniably men and women, with all the qualities of human beings—threatened not only the uneasy consciences of the slave holders but the system of slavery itself, the basis of their comfortable livelihoods. As the slave Negro became commercially more valuable, the free Negro, particularly the successful free Negro, seemed even more of a threat, and quickly became an object of hate. This was true in the North as well as in the South because profits from Southern plantations were entwined with those of shipping and other industries in the North.

All this was quite clear to Forten the sailmaker who early in his life realized that no Negro could consider himself truly free while one remained a slave.

The fourth stream of hate poured from the activities of the fast-growing American Colonization Society. Across the nation, Colonization speakers, often with humane intent, declared that there could be no happy future for the Negro in the United States. Some few lecturers openly stated that the Negro would never be able to achieve equality with the white population; that when he was free, he would be merely a nuisance and a danger to the country. Other speakers adhered to Paul Cuffe's philosophy that the Negro was a competent person, as capable as any of building and enjoying a modern, independent nation, and should be given technical and financial aid to do so.

Colonizationists of all varieties believed in freeing the Negro from slavery, but they thought emancipation should be a gradual process, one that would not disrupt the economy of the Southern states.

To a proud man like James Forten the statements and implications of some of the Colonizationists were unforgivable. His resentment was hot. He often quoted not only Jefferson's "firebell" remark, but an earlier one, "I tremble for my country when I remember that God is just, and his justice will not sleep forever."

To make matters worse, during this period of his life Forten had no white friend who could lift his spirit. Even the sympathetic Roberts Vaux, a Quaker and the President of the Philadelphia school board, and for years a Forten family friend, said gloomily: "The policy and power of the national and state governments are against them. . . . The small degree of compassion once cherished toward them in the commonwealths which got rid of slavery, or which never were disfigured by it, appears to be exhausted. Their prospects either as free, or bond men, are dreary and comfortless."

"Dreary and comfortless?" Perhaps, Forten thought to himself, but not hopeless. Not hopeless enough to make a man exile himself from the nation of his birth, a nation he loved in spite of the way it treated his people.

In February, 1820, he heard that the American Colonization Society was sending eighty-eight free Negroes and three white agents to Sherbro Island, the area near Sierra Leone that the Reverend Mills had acquired from the natives in 1817.

The black colonists had been happy and proud as they sailed from New York harbor in the schooner *Elizabeth*, which had been chartered to the Society by the United States government. Many compared themselves to the brave band of settlers who, two hundred years earlier, had left the comparative safety of Europe to seek a free life in the New World. They believed the *Elizabeth* would be regarded with as much admiration as the *Mayflower* was. How proud their descendants would be, they felt, to say that *their* ancestors had been the enterprising ones, the far-seeing ones, the brave ones—the first colonists of a new nation.

But the expedition was unfortunate. The land the colonists settled on was low, sandy, unhealthy, and infertile. By the first of June the three white agents and twenty-four of the settlers were dead of African fever. The rest fled to Sierra Leone.

Reports of the difficulties of the first settlement filtered back to the United States, but other prospective Negro colonists were undaunted by these hardships. Early in 1821, another group of thirty set sail from Norfolk in the *Nautilus*, a vessel also chartered from the United States government by the Colonization Society. And at the end of March, the U. S. schooner *Augusta* sailed with a large group of emigrants. With the two expeditions went five white agents, who this time received permission from the British to take the black colonists first to the healthier and more advanced colony of Sierra Leone.

By September, three of the white agents were dead, but most of the Negro settlers had adjusted to their new home, and were thriving. But Sierra Leone, being British, was not the new homeland the Colonization Society had in mind. In the Society's opinion the former American Negroes should establish an independent colony, with ties to America, not to Britain.

In December, 1821, two men with this mission in mind dropped anchor at Sierra Leone. They were Dr. Eli Ayres, the principal agent for the American Colonization Society, and United States Navy Captain R. F. Stockton who arrived in the U. S. schooner *Alligator*. Shortly after they arrived, the two men explored the coast as far as Mesurado Bay, and approached some of the native chiefs for a grant of land.

In exchange for gunpowder, tobacco, beads, looking glasses, pipes, and brightly colored cloth, they secured a title deed to the mouth of the Mesurado River, Cape Mesurado, and some of the back country. This territory became the actual nucleus of the Republic of Liberia. The land was ceded neither to the United States government nor to the Colonization Society but to Dr. Ayres and Captain Stockton who were to keep it as a trust for the use of the "said citizens of America." The Colonization Society hoped that in time the colony would be able to stand on its own feet, a model republic for the African to admire and, one day, to imitate.

As soon as the deed for the land was signed, Dr. Ayres returned to Sierra Leone and prepared to settle the colonists on the newly ceded territory where, on April 25, 1822, the American flag was hoisted for the first time. The colony was named Liberia. Its future capital was to be called Monrovia, in honor of President James Monroe, who had great hopes for the settlement.

Soon afterward, Dr. Ayres left Africa for America and put one of the colonists, Elijah Johnson, in charge of the colony. Trouble was not long in coming. African fevers mercilessly felled one colonist after another. Hostile natives, who resented the cession of land to the American Negroes, attacked the tiny settlement. The colonists fought for their lives much as the early American settlers had fought against the Indians.

In far off Philadelphia, James Forten received word of the troubles of the Liberian pioneers. He shook his head unhappily. It was as he had feared. His people, exiled from their native land, were being driven to their deaths in a strange, unhealthy country, the helpless victims of mysterious tropical diseases and savage, primitive enemies who resented their coming. Again he asked himself what man in his right mind would willingly leave America for Africa.

He was therefore astonished one day, in the late spring of 1822, when Francis Devany, one of his brightest and most capable workmen, told him that he was quitting his job at the sail loft and emigrating to Liberia. For a moment James could only stare at the man. He had helped Devany, once a slave in South Carolina, the property of a onetime Speaker of the House of Representatives, buy his freedom. Afterward, he had taken Devany on as an apprentice and was looking forward to the time when the former slave would be a master sailmaker with a good income.

"But what will you do there, Francis?" Forten asked when he could find his voice. "Is the colony ready for a sailmaker?"

"I cannot say, sir," Devany is reported to have replied. "But in a new colony, there are opportunities of many kinds. The Colonization Agent has spoken to me of commanding a small public vessel to navigate the African coast and obtain supplies for the settlers."

The enterprising Devany sailed away shortly in the brig *Strong*, which left from Baltimore with fifty-five emigrants, a much-needed cargo of provisions, and the new agent of the Colonization Society, the Reverend Jehudi Ashmun of Vermont.

Devany had promised to write, and Forten waited eagerly for some word of the group. But before the *Strong* even reached the African coast, a terrible incident occurred in South Carolina that drove the Liberian venture temporarily from his mind.

The incident took place in Charleston, where an educated free Negro carpenter named Denmark Vesey, originally from San Domingo, planned one of the most extensive slave revolts ever recorded. For months the Vesey group had obtained and hidden arms for the purpose of murdering the entire white population of the city. Vesey, a clever and powerful speaker, quoted words of hate from the Congressional Debates on the Missouri Compromise to inflame the slaves to commit this desperate act, which was to take place on the second Monday in July.

Again, as in the Prosser uprising, a slave who could not bear to see his kind master and his family murdered warned the authorities, and the plot was foiled. Vesey, and some of the most respected free Negroes and slaves in the area, thirty-five in all, were hanged. Forty-three other Negroes, mostly free, were banished from South Carolina, where they had been making a comfortable living as skilled workers.

Reports of the Vesey affair filtered into Philadelphia and chilled James Forten's heart. His first thought was for the slaves. How empty of hope they must have been to undertake so desperate and dangerous a deed. His mind went to the free Negroes. Unhappy as their situation might be in the North, at least they did not have to resort to bloodshed to protest the wrongs done them. They could protest openly. They could hold meetings, write letters to the newspapers, petition governing officials and legislatures. Perhaps nothing would come of their protests, but at least they were granted the human right to make them.

But now what consequences, Forten asked himself, would the Vesey Conspiracy bring to the free Negro? "From bad to disastrous" was the only answer he could come up with. The fact that the horrible massacre had been plotted by a free Negro would support those who argued that the free Negroes were dangerous to the white community; that to protect the white population the free Negroes should be deported to Africa. "Vesey," "Vesey." In his mind's ear James Forten could hear the Colonization Society speakers spitting out this name from one end of the twenty-four states to the other.

But if the Colonizationists tried to use the Vesey plot as propaganda to build their colony in Africa, such activity brought them little success. By 1824, only 225 emigrants had sailed to the African coast. Of these, no more than 140 actually lived in Liberia. Forty had died. The rest had either gone to Sierra Leone or had returned home to the United States.

Forten took little comfort in the fact that the colony was growing so slowly. The situation would change, he feared, if the United States government agreed to provide funds for sending the free Negroes to Liberia. At every session of Congress the Colonizationists managed to present a bill that would bring Federal money into the venture. But they were never successful in getting it passed.

Most Congressmen deemed such an act unconstitutional. It would, they said, mean that the Federal government was "intruding itself into the states for the purpose of withdrawing from them an important part of their population." Some Congressmen feared that the Federal government might even be called upon to pay the owners the equivalent of the price of the slaves in order to obtain their manumission. No matter how the Colonizationists argued, the Government would do no more than charter an occasional ship to the Society to carry the emigrants across the ocean.

But if the Federal government did little to encourage the free Negroes to emigrate to Africa, it also did little to encourage them in their homeland. It kept a closed-mouth policy when the states enacted new hardship regulations for Negroes.

In 1824, Virginia passed a law stating that anyone assisting a slave to escape would be imprisoned for a year; that anyone teaching free Negroes to read and write would be imprisoned for two months and fined fifty dollars.

Slave ships still plied their illegal and ugly trade and smuggled newly stolen Africans into the slave-holding states. Some of these slavers were intercepted by government patrols, but many were able to carry out their evil mission. Everywhere the slave-catchers grew bolder. In Philadelphia, along the river front, not far from Forten's sail loft, an increasing number of Negro children were kidnapped, taken by boat to cotton plantations in the South, and often never heard from again.

Toward the end of September, Forten's spirits rose, for a great humanitarian hero came to Philadelphia, bringing with him memories of the idealism that had shone across America during the Revolution. Lafayette, as the Nation's Guest, had come back to tour in triumph the young nation that he had helped bring into existence almost half a century earlier.

All the city was bright with flags and banners, joyous with music and the cheers of the crowds as the tall French nobleman, now sixty-seven years old, rode ceremoniously through the streets. Never before had any foreigner been given such a reception, and none has since then. Uniformed bands, carriages of leading citizens, elaborate floats escorted Lafayette's barouche to Independence Hall where he was to be welcomed.

Every night there was a banquet in his honor. Every afternoon there was a reception for him in Independence Hall. Obviously Lafayette had little time to himself. Yet one morning he slipped away alone and went on foot to a poor part of the city near the waterfront. He entered one of the smallest houses and smilingly presented a gift to the aged woman who lived there. She was, in the words of a Philadelphia newspaper, "Mrs. Hannah Till, a black woman who had been cook to General Washington and General Lafayette in all their campaigns during the War of Independence."

Forten was not surprised by Lafayette's kind action. Since the days of the Revolution the Frenchman had been an especial friend of the Negro people. In 1788 he was a founder of the Society of the Friends of The Blacks (*Les Amis des Noirs*), an organization that worked for the emancipation of Negro slaves everywhere. Now in 1824, as he toured through the fast-growing United States, his heart was reported to be heavy when he found that slavery was still a stain, an even larger and darker stain than before, upon the brightness of the American shield.

In 1825, before returning to France, Lafayette came back to Philadelphia for a few days. While he was there a shameful incident occurred, one that the great-hearted Frenchman undoubtedly heard of with sorrow.

One chilly night several young white hoodlums entered Bethel Church, where the venerable Richard Allen was preaching, and threw a mixture of cayenne pepper and salt on the heated stove. Soon irritating fumes spread through the crowded room. The congregation coughed, sneezed, and found breathing difficult. Suddenly a voice shouted "Fire!" Panic seized the churchgoers, and they stampeded toward the door. In the rush hundreds of persons were thrown to the floor. Dozens were trod upon. One woman died as she was removed from the heap of fallen bodies. Another succumbed the next day. Several were so severely injured that they died later. The hoodlums, although they could be identified, were not arrested or punished in any way.

This unconcern of the legal authorities is what most disturbed Forten and the entire Negro community. As time went on, unpunished lawlessness increased in Philadelphia. From isolated acts of hoodlumism grew fearful and uncontrolled riots.

13

This Vehement Man, This Garrison

Would the winter storms never end? Forten eyed the sleet beating against the window of his sail loft. He peered out toward the bay where the howling winds tossed the vessels about as though they were twigs swirling in a creek. It was now the fifteenth of January, 1827. For over two weeks there had been no let-up in the icy gales that nearly paralyzed the city. In the ice-filled river and bay, sixty-two vessels, heavy with cargo, had been driven out to sea. Reports of broken ships and of seriously injured and frost-bitten seamen came daily to those whose businesses lay along the waterfront.

Forten took no comfort in the knowledge that the thousands of sails damaged by the storms meant increased business for him. He worried about the hardships the severe weather was inflicting upon the poorer members of the Negro community. As memories of his own poverty-filled boyhood flooded over him, he asked Charlotte to keep an enormous pot of nourishing soup simmering in the kitchen fireplace. The girls—Margaretta, Sarah, Harriet, and Mary—were told to serve steaming bowls of it to anyone who came to the door hungry.

Then, as suddenly as they had come, the icy gales ceased, the snowstorms ended, the sun shone palely, and Philadelphians basked in a foretaste of spring. To Forten, even more welcome than the soft breezes was some information he received from New York City. The black people, he heard, were to have their own weekly newspaper, *Freedom's Journal*, written and published entirely by members of their race. Its editors were to be John B. Russwurm and Samuel Cornish. Forten knew and admired Cornish, a Presbyterian minister who had been educated in Philadelphia. He had heard of the twenty-six-year-old Russwurm, who had been born in Jamaica and educated in Canada. In 1826 Russwurm had graduated from Bowdoin College in Maine to become the first Negro college graduate in the United States. At Bowdoin he had become a good friend of another student, who encouraged him in his dream of a Negro newspaper, a young writer named Nathaniel Hawthorne.

The first issue of *Freedom's Journal* appeared on March 16, 1827. James looked at it eagerly and, with a feeling of pride, noticed its professional appearance—fourteen pages, and bound like a fine magazine. "Righteousness Exalteth a Nation." He read the *Journal's* motto with an approving nod of his head. The leading article—an account of the life of Paul Cuffe—brought a touch of sadness, for James still missed his friend. He settled down to read the first Negro newspaper's first editorial.

"We wish to plead our own cause," it began. "Too long have others spoken for us. . . . Our vices and our degradation are ever arrayed against us, but our virtues are passed by unnoticed."

Forten went over the long presentation carefully. The *Journal* considered education of the highest importance to the Negro people. It proposed to "urge upon our brethren the necessity of training their children, while young, to habits of industry, and thus forming them for becoming useful members of society."

The *Journal* considered the civil rights of the black people of the utmost value. It proposed to bring to public attention cases of Negroes deprived of their civil rights. It urged Negroes, who were qualified by laws in certain states, to vote

—and to vote independently. "We wish them not to become tools of party."

Freedom's Journal wanted the black people to be proud of their African heritage. "Useful knowledge of every kind and everything that relates to Africa shall find a ready admission into our columns; and as that vast continent becomes daily more known, we trust that many things will come to light, proving that the natives of it are neither so ignorant nor stupid as they have generally been supposed to be."

The *Journal* hoped that Negroes from all sections of the nation would use its pages to communicate with each other and thus strengthen the natural bond between them.

There was good sense and truth in Russwurm's views, Forten concluded. Actually he felt that he himself had been trying to carry out these purposes for most of his life. Take education. Ever since he had returned from his year in England, in 1786, he had held free classes, first in his home and later in St. Thomas Church, to teach Negro children to read, write, and cipher.

He had kept on with this work even after 1818 when the State of Pennsylvania opened its first public schools, for Negro children were not permitted to attend the new schools with white children, and no money had been allotted for Negro schools. Not until 1822, when the Pennsylvania Abolition Society donated a school building and persuaded the state to supply the teachers for a school in Philadelphia, had the busy fifty-six-year-old sailmaker given up his volunteer teaching.

As the months passed, especially after Cornish withdrew from the venture, Forten grew disappointed with *Freedom's Journal*. For one thing there was not as much news from the Philadelphia Negro community as he would have liked.

Occasionally, however, accounts appeared of pioneer experiments in education which the Philadelphia Negroes were carrying out. One of Forten's favorite experiments—which would today be called a Head Start Program—was the Infant School for Coloured Children, sponsored by the Infant School Society, of which Forten was a leading member, in May, 1828. An unsigned article in *Freedom's Journal* stated:

> It is a notorious fact that the minds of many of our children are so corrupted previous to entering school, from the bad example daily set before them, both at home and abroad, that the year or two which they spend so irregularly within the walls of a schoolhouse profit them but little. The Infant School Society, aware of this, have resolved to receive children at two years ... into their school. So far the Society has been eminently successful not only in procuring a well-qualified Instructress and Assistant but also in having as many pupils as they could conveniently seat and instruct.

What worried Forten most about the *Journal* was the increasing number of items devoted to Liberia. Favorable accounts they were, too. He wondered whether John Russwurm was becoming a Colonizationist. Forten fervently hoped not.

In March, 1829, his uneasiness about Russwurm's attitude toward colonization was justified. The young editor stopped publishing *Freedom's Journal*, and emigrated to Liberia himself. There he established a school system for the colony, founded the first newspaper, *The Liberia Herald*, and later became Governor of the Liberian province of Maryland.

About the time that John Russwurm was sailing to Liberia, a balding, twenty-four-year-old man was released from a Baltimore jail to which he had been sentenced for libeling a Boston shipowner as a slave trader. The man's name was William Lloyd Garrison. In a few years his fearless, almost fanatical, hatred of slavery and of slave owners and his inflammatory words were to affect the life of every Negro and almost every white person in the United States. But in June of 1829,

James Forten, whose life was to be significantly intertwined with Garrison's, had never heard of him.

He *had* heard of Benjamin Lundy, the brave little Quaker saddler who in 1821 had founded the antislavery paper, *The Genius of Universal Emancipation* which he published in various places as he moved about the country looking for work. It was Lundy who, in 1828, had interested Garrison, then a printer in Boston, in the antislavery cause. Garrison had also had newspaper experience. At the age of twenty-one he had been editor and publisher of the Newburyport (Mass.) *Free Press*, in which he published the first poems of nineteen-year-old John Greenleaf Whittier. The paper soon failed, but Whittier, who was to become a noted poet, remained Garrison's lifelong friend.

In 1829, Lundy set up his paper in Baltimore, and Garrison went there to assist him. Garrison's views soon proved too extreme for Lundy. The two men had already decided to part when Garrison was jailed. Neither Garrison nor Lundy had the money to pay Garrison's fine. He languished in jail for seven weeks until Arthur Tappan, a wealthy New York merchant, the grand-nephew of Benjamin Franklin, and an ardent foe of slavery, sent the money for his release.

While he had been in jail, Garrison had spent a lot of time thinking about the slavery question. He knew nothing of this evil first hand, for he had never been farther south than Baltimore. Nor did he really know any Negroes. From this point of ignorance he was inclined to agree with those white persons who considered the Negro as an inferior being, unable to achieve equality with the white population. He also believed with the Colonizationists that a return to the African homeland was the best solution to the black man's problems. But the fact that he held these views did not interfere with his firm belief that slavery itself was wicked, vicious, and immoral, a practice that must be cut out from the nation's body, if that body were to survive.

To fight this evil, Garrison decided to publish an antislavery paper of his own. His paper, he determined, would not be like Lundy's—gentle and moderate. His paper would speak with a loud, forceful voice that no one could ignore. The fact that he had no money for such a venture did not discourage him in the least. As he made his way back to Boston after leaving the jail, he impressed people who saw him as a man in a terrific rush.

"I am," he said to those who would listen. "I have a system to destroy, and I have no time to waste."

No newspaper can run on good intentions, a fact that William Lloyd Garrison, who had already failed in two publishing ventures, knew well. A newspaper must have some money behind it, and he at the moment was practically penniless. The hand-to-mouth existence of Lundy's antislavery paper was a perfect example of the difficulties a journal, published solely to promote a humanitarian cause, must overcome. He had already decided that *his* paper would feature articles and essays from Negroes as well as from white antislavery workers. The more he thought about this aspect of his prospective publication, the more he was convinced that Negroes would be willing to help in financing it.

In 1830 Garrison knew that of the free Negro groups in the United States, New York City's was the largest, with 14,000 people. Philadelphia came next with 9,700. Garrison's own city of Boston had less than 2,000. The Philadelphia group was the best educated, the most public spirited, and the richest. And of this group James Forten, sailmaker, was the best known, not only for helping his people but also for his intelligence, integrity, energy, inventiveness, and hard work, by which he had amassed probably the largest fortune of any Negro in the United States.

As he considered these facts, Garrison decided to write this eminent man and ask for his help in establishing a newspaper that would devote itself primarily to freeing the slaves, but also to improving the condition of the free Negroes. He had already chosen a name for his paper—*The Liberator.*

When Forten received Garrison's letter, he was busy with other matters. He put it aside to answer when he could give it his full attention. Just when this would be, he could not say, for week after week brought some event that took his time and thoughts. In May, Francis Devany, his former employee, returned home in triumph from Liberia. Devany had long since given up his trade of sailmaker, and was now the High Sheriff of the American colony on Africa's west coast. He was also rich.

Shortly after he had arrived in Liberia he was employed by the Colonization Agent to sail a small vessel along the coast to obtain supplies for the settlers at Monrovia. Devany soon sized up the opportunities and established a shipping business of his own. Now in his own brig *Liberia*, with a cargo worth $20,000, he had come back to Philadelphia to visit his relatives. He did not stay long, for he had been summoned to Washington to testify before a Committee of Congress on conditions in the colony.

Naturally Devany's visit strengthened the Colonizationists' argument that the Negro people would find greater opportunity in Africa than they ever could in America, but Forten remained unconvinced. Always he kept the thought: we are Americans, born here, knowing only American traditions and ways. Many of us fought to free this nation from tyranny. Why should the color of our skin force us to leave our own land? Why should we not have the same opportunity to succeed here as other groups who have come to these shores?

Still, Devany's visit worried him. He was relieved when Congress decided again that the United States government could not support a colony in Africa. Liberia would have to carry on as before—the project of a private group, the American Colonization Society.

From time to time Forten considered Garrison's proposed *Liberator,* and his thoughts went back to Russwurm's *Freedom's Journal.* The *Journal* had had one important result. It had given its readers a feeling of "togetherness." It had made them realize that the problem of one black man was often the problem of all. Out of this realization grew the conviction that it would be helpful for the free Negroes from all over the United States to meet together and discuss these problems.

By the middle of September, 1830, this conviction was converted into action. Leading free Negroes from seven states —Pennsylvania, New York, Connecticut, Rhode Island, Maryland, Delaware, and Virginia—gathered in Reverend Richard Allen's church in Philadelphia to think together. In the pulpit, Allen, his long hair white, his kindly face seamed with age, told the delegates in a surprisingly strong voice:

> Brethren,
> ... our forlorn and deplorable situation earnestly and loudly demands of us to devise and pursue all legal means for the speedy elevation of ourselves and our brethren to the scale and standing of men.

Just what these legal means were to be—or could be— the delegates to this Pioneer Negro Convention were not as yet prepared to say. All still burned with anger at what had happened recently in Cincinnati, Ohio. Here a mob of white hoodlums had attacked the free Negroes and burned their homes, so that nearly two thousand of them were forced to flee ever northward until they reached Canada where they at last found refuge. Even more resented by the delegates was the official endorsement by the Pennsylvania Legislature of the Colonization movement, an ultimate threat, they felt, to each man present.

After a few days of discussion—without decisions—the delegates went home. They vowed to return to Philadelphia the next June, with more delegates from more cities. By that time they hoped to have some definite plan that would help their people out of their increasing difficulties.

James, who had been instrumental in setting up the Convention, shook hands with each departing delegate and thanked him for coming. As he gazed into the alert, earnest, and intelligent faces, he felt a surge of hope. Here indeed were men whose own triumph over the hardships and handicaps of racial prejudice could serve as a torch to light the path to freedom and acceptance for all Negroes.

After the delegates left, Forten gave his attention to Garrison's proposed antislavery newspaper. He liked what Garrison had written to him; and the fact that Garrison had been associated with the humane Lundy was enough to win Forten's confidence.

On December 15, 1830 he wrote to Garrison:

> I am extremely happy to hear that you are about establishing a paper in Boston. I hope your efforts may not be in vain; and may the "Liberator" be the means of exposing more and more, the odious system of Slavery, and of raising up friends to the oppressed and degraded People of Colour throughout the Union. Whilst so much is doing in the world, to ameliorate the condition of mankind, and the spirit of Freedom is marching with rapid strides, and causing tyrants to tremble, may America awake from the apathy in which she has long slumbered.

With his letter, Forten enclosed the money for twenty-seven subscriptions, the first of his many contributions to the editor.

In Boston on New Year's Day, 1831, young Mr. Garrison, who had to use borrowed paper and borrowed type, published the first issue of the *Liberator*.

In Philadelphia a few days later Forten scanned the four small pages. OUR COUNTRY IS THE WORLD—OUR

Masthead of The Liberator

COUNTRYMEN ARE MANKIND proclaimed the banner across the top of page one. The salutation at the head of the first column declared:

> My name is Liberator! I propose
> To hurl my shafts at freedom's deadliest foes!
> My task is hard—for I am charged to save
> *Man from his brother*—to redeem the slave!

Since the leading editorial of a newspaper, particularly of a first issue, reveals the editor's mind and policy, Forten read this feature first. He read:

> I shall strenuously contend for the immediate en-franchisement of our slave population.... I will be as harsh as truth, and as uncompromising as justice. On this subject I do not wish to think, speak, or write with moderation. No! No! Tell a man whose house is on fire, to give a moderate alarm ... tell the mother to gradually extricate her babe from the fire into which it has fallen —but urge me not to use moderation in a cause like the present. I am in earnest—I will not equivocate—I will not excuse—I will not retreat a single inch—and I will be heard.

Forten must have felt a mental gasp for breath as he read

Garrison's words. The whole paper breathed of a fire and storm, of a passionate concern he had never heard from a white man for the Negro's plight. *Immediate freeing* of the slaves. All slaves. This was a startling thought. The earlier humanitarians like Rush, Benezet, Franklin, and Jefferson, the kindly white friends he had now in Philadelphia, had never proposed so drastic a measure. Certainly the slaves should be freed, they said, but gradually, so that the shock to the economic system of the nation would not be so great.

Forten thoughtfully smoothed the small paper in his hands. He had always believed in appealing to the laws of the land and to the better side of human nature. He still believed in these things. But perhaps this vehement man, this Garrison, who like himself had been born in poverty and had been forced to work at the age of nine, could rouse the nation from its apathy toward the Negro, where calmer spirits had failed. Perhaps the strident voice, the militancy of William Lloyd Garrison were what the United States needed.

14

Caught
in the Cross Fire

At the age of sixty-five, Forten the sailmaker had the vigor and zest of a healthy man of forty. In 1831 he channeled much of this energy and enthusiasm into helping William Lloyd Garrison and his *Liberator*. He sent money. He gathered subscriptions. He called meetings of the Philadelphia Negroes to explain and endorse the paper. He wrote encouraging letters that Garrison was glad to publish in the newspaper's columns. Sarah and James Jr., catching fire from their father's enthusiasm, sent in writings of their own.

Sarah, particularly, attracted considerable attention by her poems, which appeared under her own name and under the pen name of Ada. In April, 1831, Forten proudly read her poem, "The Slave."

> Our sires who once in freedom's cause
> Their boasted freedom sought and won,
> For deeds of glory gained applause,
> When patriot feeling led them on.
>
> And can their sons now speak with pride,
> Of rights for which they bled and died....
> The sweets of freedom now they know,
> They care not for the captive's woe.
>
> The poor wronged slave can bear no part
> In feelings dearest to his heart.
> He cannot speak on freedom's side,
> Nor dare he own a freeman's pride.

His soul is dark, ay dark as night
On which is shed no gleam of light. . . .

To know that his is doomed to be
A life, and death, of slavery.
But will not justice soon arise
And plead the cause of the despised?
Oh! My Country, must it be,
That they still find a foe in thee?

In June Garrison came to Philadelphia. He had been invited, along with three other white friends of the Negro people, to attend the First Annual Negro Convention. Forten looked at all the white men with interest. He gazed at five-foot-tall Benjamin Lundy, at kind-faced Arthur Tappan, at the Reverend Jocelyn, who was home missionary to a Negro congregation in New Haven. His eyes stayed longest on Garrison—tall, thin, bald, eyes glowing behind his spectacles, and seeming older than his twenty-six years.

Garrison returned the sailmaker's steady gaze with a searching and slightly surprised stare of his own. Then with a warm, impulsive gesture, the editor reached out both his hands in a grasp of friendship. To James Forten this meeting was "a green spot in the desert of life." To Garrison it was a revelation. In later years he credited James Forten with proving to him that the Negro race was not inferior to the white. He also said that it was Forten who first convinced him that colonization was not in the interest of the American black man, whether slave or free.

At the convention the eyes of the delegates must have rested affectionately upon James Forten. He was the only one left of the original great Negro leaders in America, for Richard Allen had died in March. But Forten was more interested in the Negro's future in the United States than in his past. He heard with satisfaction the report concerning the two thousand Negroes who had been driven from their Ohio homes to Canada. They were now well established in Ontario where they had bought eight hundred acres of good farmland and had already built two hundred houses upon it.

When the discussion turned from the exiles to the Negroes in the United States, Forten proposed something he had dreamed of for years. This was a self-supporting college that would prepare young black men for the mechanical and agricultural trades, and would at the same time give them a classical education.

The Convention quickly approved the idea and set about raising the money for the institution. The delegates also selected the site for the college—New Haven, Connecticut. "It is ideal," declared the Reverend Jocelyn, "because of its literary and scientific fame, its central location, the liberality of state laws, and the friendly, pious, generous, and humane character of its residents."

Possibly the residents of New Haven would have shown their "friendly, generous, and humane character," had not the entire nation been horrified by an event that took place in Virginia on a hot, quiet Sunday in August, 1831. On that day Nat Turner, a thirty-one-year-old slave on a Southampton County farm, led an uprising in which about seventy slaves roamed the area and slaughtered every white man, woman, child (about sixty in all) they came upon. Most of the participants in the revolt were quickly arrested, tried, and hanged, although Turner himself was not captured and executed until November.

The Turner insurrection was quickly blamed upon the activities of the Abolitionists, particularly upon the *Liberator*, whose militant statements about immediate emancipation were thought to encourage the slaves to take matters into their own hands.

Most Southern states swiftly passed laws placing further restrictions upon both slaves and free Negroes. In the North a wave of fear and hostility flowed over communities that previously had shown sympathy for the black man's plight. Instead of welcoming the proposed Negro college, the citizens of New Haven crowded into a town meeting and, by a vote of 700 to 4, angrily forbade the college to locate there.

In Pennsylvania the Turner uprising made many citizens openly fear all black people and not want them around. This concern caused the Pennsylvania Assembly to pass two Resolutions. The first was to look into the passage of a law "to protect the citizens of this commonwealth against the evils arising from the emigration of free blacks from other states into Pennsylvania." The other Resolution asked that the State repeal its own fugitive slave law and use instead the Federal Fugitive Slave Act of 1793, which was harsher toward the escaped slave.

Forten the sailmaker felt very old and very tired when he learned of the Assembly's action; but when his people called to him for help, as they always did, he could not ignore their cries. In January of 1832, the old war-horse called a meeting of the Philadelphia Negroes. At their insistence he drafted a petition of protest to the Legislature. This time he had the aid of two brilliant young men "of color," William Whipper, and his own son-in-law, Robert Purvis, who had recently married his daughter Harriet.

This petition, like earlier ones, reminded the legislators of the great tradition of humanity and justice in Pennsylvania toward the black man, and asked:

> Why is this distinction now to be proclaimed for the first time in the code of Pennsylvania? Why are her borders to be surrounded by a wall of iron against freemen whose complexions fall below the wavering and uncertain shades of white....? It is not to be asked, is he brave—is he honest—is he just—is he free from the stain of crime——but is he black—is he brown—is he yellow—is he other than white....

The Negroes denied that they had in any way encouraged the Nat Turner massacre. "They repel the slander," wrote Forten. "As children of the state, they look to it as a guardian and a protector, and in common with you feel the necessity of maintaining law and order. . . ."

"Equally unfounded is the charge," the Philadelphia Negroes emphasized, "that this population fills the almshouses with paupers—and increases, in an undue proportion, the public burdens. We appeal to the facts and documents which accompany this memorial, as giving abundant refutation to an error so injurious to our character."

Forten had spent hours gathering these "facts and documents" from public records, which were open to all. They showed a number of things: that the people of color paid more taxes on their property than the amount of public funds spent on the Negro poor; that Negroes in the city owned over one hundred thousand dollars in real estate value; that they had over fifty societies of their own to help each other in times of sickness and need. The documents showed also that Negroes who could manage it sent their children to school at their own expense, and that black people were trying hard to rise from the unskilled to the skilled labor group. Despite the difficulty, stated the petition, of "getting places for our sons as apprentices to learn the mechanical trades, owing to the prejudices with which we have to contend, there are between four and five hundred people of color in the city and suburbs who follow mechanical employments."

Negroes are no different from other men, Forten had concluded. Like those of a different color,

> . . . we are liable to be drawn aside by temptation from the paths of rectitude. But we think that in the aggregate we will not suffer by a comparison with our white neighbors whose opportunities of improvement have been no

greater than ours. By such a comparison, fairly and im-
partially made, we are willing to be judged.

Perhaps the undeniable logic in Forten's petition swayed
the legislators. Perhaps the proposed Resolutions appeared not
only unenforceable but extremely cruel. In any case, they
were not passed, and the Pennsylvania Negroes were spared
this humiliation. But the black people's situation did not improve. Instead, month by month, it grew bewilderingly worse.

The Abolitionists felt the Colonizationists were mainly to
blame for this state of affairs. On the other hand many people
blamed the Abolitionists themselves for the growing Negro
difficulties. These reformers, they said, were so irritating and
so unreasonable in their zeal to bring immediate freedom to
the slave that they aroused anger and resentment in the North
as well as in the South. Their "wild statements" stirred up
antagonism toward the black man where none had existed
before.

Caught between the cross fire of these two battling groups,
the unfortunate Negroes, both slave and free, found little
peace.

In Philadelphia, where important groups of colonizationists and abolitionists existed, and free Negroes flocked to com-
pete with the ever-increasing flood of immigrants, the situation
was often described as a tinderbox. In August, 1832, the tinderbox exploded.

It began at an amusement park where whites and blacks
got into an argument over the horses at the merry-go-round.
When word spread that the blacks had insulted the whites, a
large party of young white men from the outskirts of the city
flocked to the park and started to fight with the Negroes. In
the melee the merry-go-round and several other buildings were
totally destroyed. The white hoodlums then ran off.

The next day the whole city was in an uproar over the
disturbance. At night, a far greater crowd, mostly boys and

young men armed with clubs, gathered near the Pennsylvania Hospital, where they were joined by other ruffians.

From this area the mob ran to the Negro section of the city and began to break windows, batter down doors, and force their way into the houses where they seized the furniture and flung it into the streets for other hoodlums to smash into bits. Negroes whenever caught were beaten mercilessly.

The rioters were finally put to flight by the arrival of two divisions of city police, headed by Mayor Swift, who marched upon the mob and took numerous prisoners. The next day three hundred special constables were sworn in. The City Troop and the Washington Grays [similar to today's National Guard] were ordered under arms and remained at the armories all night. Special posses assembled and marched to the scenes of previous disturbances.

Meanwhile excitement arose in another part of town where rumors started that Negroes had fired upon several young white boys walking past a Negro meetinghouse. A mob soon collected, tore down the meetinghouse, attacked eight Negro homes, and set fire to a Negro church. The posse arrived, and the mob was broken up.

These hoodlum-inspired riots ceased at midnight, but the next day Irish laborers employed in the coal-yards on the Schuylkill attacked Negro laborers at work nearby. The sheriff sent out a posse of sixty men. These were attacked by the mob and forced to flee, leaving the field to the rioters who, by then almost insane in their frenzy, raced to other sections of the city and attacked every Negro they could find.

Fearful of what the night might bring, the sheriff begged for and got troops in great strength. These, armed with loaded muskets and pieces of artillery, were stationed in strategic parts of Philadelphia. The presence of the soldiers discouraged the mobs until at least a surface calm returned to the frightened city.

Shocked and alarmed by the race riots, city officials made

investigations and appointed committees to try to prevent their reoccurrence. But they were helpless in combating the underlying causes of the trouble—the influx of freedmen, escaped slaves, and immigrants into a city that was not prepared to provide work or social acceptance for them. Many of Philadelphia's hard-working, self-respecting Negroes became bitter. They felt that their white friends, even the Quakers, had deserted them.

Forten did not go along with the bitter ones. In a nation where every voice may be heard, he told his friends, there are times when the voices of the mean and violent outshout those of reason and humanity.

In Forten's opinion, one voice crying out in powerful and convincing tones for justice to the Negro was that of William Lloyd Garrison. Unfortunately, word had come from Boston that Garrison's voice was weakening for lack of money. The editor had spent much of the funds allotted to the *Liberator* on a book called *Thoughts on Colonization*, which was to be published in the fall of 1832.

James awaited this book with keen interest. He had given Garrison many of the ideas for it, and he was eager to see what the abolitionist had done with them.

Garrison's *Thoughts on Colonization* turned out to be a more powerful weapon against the American Colonization Society than the most ardent abolitionist had hoped for. The ministers who attempted to carry the message of colonization throughout the land were no match for Garrison's zeal, his masterful arguments, and his immense talent for subtle ridicule.

James quickly perceived the power of *Thoughts on Colonization*. He bought and distributed hundreds of copies throughout Pennsylvania. The profits from the sale of these books sent a timely flow of money to the *Liberator* office, from which Garrison wrote to Robert Purvis in December:

The just man shall be in eternal remembrance

Went to prison for Teaching Colored Children.

Prudence Crandall

You will please convey to your noble father-in-law all that hearts filled with gratitude may be supposed to utter. . . .The extraordinary purchase of so large a number of copies of our *Thoughts* in Philadelphia has given us material assistance. . . . Already we are able to assure you there is no cause for apprehension in regard to the continuance of the *Liberator*.

Although over three-fourths of the *Liberator's* subscribers were Negro, the paper did have a few white readers. One of these was a beautiful twenty-three-year-old Quaker school teacher named Prudence Crandall. In 1831, Prudence had opened a boarding school for girls in the charming little town of Canterbury, Connecticut. The school prospered for more than a year. Then Prudence admitted an intelligent mulatto girl from the town who wished to become a teacher so that she might instruct colored children.

Immediately there were protests from the townspeople. Most of the white parents withdrew their daughters. "Your school will—and should—fail," the wife of the Episcopal minister told her angrily. Shocked and indignant, Prudence wrote Garrison, asking his advice about changing her school into one entirely for Negro girls. Garrison thought her idea a good one, and praised her courage.

At Garrison's urging, she placed this notice in the Liberator:

> Prudence Crandall, Principal of Canterbury (Conn.) Female Boarding School announces that on Monday of April next, her school will be opened for the reception of young Ladies and little Misses of Color. Branches taught will be Reading, Writing, Arithmetic, English Grammar, Geography, History, Natural and Moral Philosophy, Chemistry, Astronomy, Drawing, Painting, Music on the Piano, together with the French language. Terms, including board, washing, and tuition—$25 per quarter.
> For information respecting the school, reference may be made to the following gentlemen.

Prudence's references in Philadelphia were Joseph Cassey, a wealthy wigmaker, and James Forten.

The advertisement in the Liberator threw Canterbury into a near panic. The town officials tried to persuade Prudence to give up the idea, declaring that it would bring "injurious effects and incalculable evils" to the community. But Prudence, now backed not only by Garrison but by other outspoken abolitionists, both white and Negro, opened her school on schedule. She was proud of her students, who came from many places. Several of them, such as Elizabeth Douglass Bustill of Philadelphia, the granddaughter of Cyrus Bustill, were descendants of men who had fought with George Washington in the Revolution.

Unfortunately, none of the girls, who were reported to be intelligent and well-mannered, could attend Prudence's school long enough to graduate. The townspeople declared immediate war against them. The girls dared not step outside the school, for a vagrancy law under which outsiders might be given ten lashes on a bare back had been invoked.

> Shops and meeting house were closed against teacher and pupils. Not a shop in town would sell her [Miss Crandall] a morsel of food; carriage in a public conveyance was denied to them, physicians would not call; the school well was filled with manure, and water from other sources was refused to them; the house was smeared with filth, assailed with rotten eggs and stones, and finally set on fire.

In May the State of Connecticut hurriedly passed a law that forbade the establishment of any school, academy, or literary institution for the instruction of colored persons who were not inhabitants of the state. Her school was now illegal, but Prudence refused to close it down. She was arrested, and refusing bail from prominent abolitionists, stayed in jail overnight to call attention to her persecution and to an unjust law. The *Liberator* headlined her case and published weekly editorials in her defense. When Prudence came to trial, her expenses were paid by Arthur Tappan, and she was defended by Samuel J. May, a young Unitarian minister, the uncle of Louisa May Alcott. May defended her ably, but Prudence

Samuel J. May

was convicted. Later, when her conviction was reversed in a higher court, a mob gathered on the village green, marched on the school, broke all the windows, and physically threatened the pupils.

As Prudence looked at the trembling young Negro girls trying hard to be brave, she concluded that to save them from actual harm she had better close her school.

Distressing as the Prudence Crandall affair was to James Forten, he was able to extract some encouragement from it. As a result of the incident, people who heretofore had not given the matter much thought were openly expressing sympathy for the Negro. Garrison was quick to take advantage of this sentiment. In September, 1833, the *Liberator* called for a National Anti-Slavery Convention to be held in Philadelphia in December. Owing to the editor's tireless zeal, the meeting was arranged with surprising speed.

On a raw gray Wednesday, the fourth of December, sixty-two delegates from ten states gathered in Philadelphia. Most of them were very young, and most were very poor. "Without influence or position ... little known, strong only in their convictions and faith in the justice of their cause ... all had the earnestness which might be expected of men engaged in an enterprise beset with difficulty, perhaps with peril," was how the twenty-six-year-old poet, John Greenleaf Whittier, described his fellow delegates.

The rich, fashionable Philadelphia Quakers pointedly ignored them, and the police insisted that their meetings in Adelphi Hall must end before nightfall. "Your kind is not liked here," the officials told them. "After dark we cannot guarantee you protection from the mobs."

15

Visitors
of Importance

Forten the sailmaker did not attend the organization meeting of the American Anti-Slavery Society. Perhaps at sixty-seven he felt he was too old. But his son-in-law, twenty-three-year-old Robert Purvis, played a leading role in the convention. When, on the first day of the gathering, Purvis rose to "utter heartfelt thanks to the delegates who had convened for the deliverance of my people," a murmur rose within the hall. The delegates craned their necks to see the speaker. Most of them appeared to agree with Whittier, who wrote of Purvis, "Never have I seen a finer face and figure, and his manner, words, and bearing are in keeping."

But why, many delegates wondered, did this fair-skinned, brown-haired man call himself a Negro? Who was he really? James Forten had put these same questions to Purvis before he gave his consent to the young man to marry his daughter Harriet.

Purvis had answered truthfully. His father was a well-to-do English merchant who had settled in Charleston, South Carolina. His mother was of German-Moroccan extraction with a small amount of Negro blood. At the age of twelve she had been kidnapped in Morocco and sold into American slavery, but was freed before her marriage. When Robert was nine, the Purvis family moved to Philadelphia. All the Purvis children were well educated. Robert himself had attended Amherst College.

As to why he considered himself a Negro, Robert said simply that since in the United States any known amount of Negro blood made a man a Negro, he preferred it this way. He had dedicated his energies, his inherited wealth, and the considerable income from his magnificent farm at nearby Byberry to the cause of freedom for the slave and equal rights with other Americans for the free Negro. Perhaps, Purvis told Forten, his white appearance would be an extra weapon in his fight for justice to the black man.

Robert Purvis was not the only Negro delegate to the organization meeting of the American Anti-Slavery Society. Three other prominent black men—James McCrummel, a Philadelphia dentist; James Vashon, a businessman; and Abraham Shadd of Delaware also took part in the proceedings.

At the end of the first day, as the early winter dark crept into the windows of the meeting hall, the convention president, the Reverend Beriah Green of Oneida Institute, New York, appointed William Lloyd Garrison, the Reverend S. J. May, and John G. Whittier to draft a Declaration of Principles for the new society.

Garrison, the most powerful writer of the three, agreed to compose the first draft. "We agreed to meet him at his lodgings in the home of a colored friend [James McCrummel] early the next day," wrote Whittier. "It was early gray morning when we climbed up to the small upper chamber, and the lamp was still burning, by the light of which he was writing the last sentence of the Declaration."

Bleary-eyed and pale with fatigue, Garrison handed the paper he had worked on through the night to the Reverend May with the comment, "Bear in mind, we have to undo the accumulated wrongs of two centuries and remake the manhood which slavery has well-nigh unmade."

On Thursday morning the Convention gathered to hear the reading of the Declaration of Principles of the American Anti-Slavery Society. Outside the circle of delegates sat a number of keenly interested spectators. Among them were Lucretia Mott, beautiful and graceful in her simple Quaker gray gown and bonnet; her husband James; Edward Abdy, an Englishman sent over by Parliament to study the American prison system; Robert Gurley, Secretary of the American Colonization Society; Benjamin Lundy; and three of James Forten's daughters, Margaretta, Sarah, and Harriet (Mrs. Robert Purvis).

All Thursday the delegates discussed the wording of the Declaration of Sentiments for the American Anti-Slavery Society. Some thought the Sentiments too strong; others that they were not strong enough. Then, as the shadows of night deepened, they all agreed on certain "significant articles," but "because of shortening daylight," wrote Garrison in after years, "the signing was put off until the next day." Garrison's report continued:

> On Friday, May's sweet, persuasive voice faltered with the intensity of his emotions as he repeated the solemn pledges of the concluding paragraphs: "To deliver our land from its deadliest curse [slavery] and to secure to the colored population all the rights and privileges which belong to them as Americans—come what may to our persons, our interests, or our reputation."
>
> As the secretaries called his name, one after another passed up to the platform, signed, and retired to silence. All felt the responsibility of the occasion—the shadow and forecast of a lifelong struggle rested on every countenance.

"Of the sixty signers of the Declaration of Sentiments," wrote another observer, "all were male; twenty-one were Quakers, and two—Robert Purvis and James McCrummel—were colored."

As the historic meeting ended, Reverend Green turned over his gavel to Arthur Tappan, the first president of the American Anti-Slavery Society, and raised his hands in a parting prayer for divine guidance for the group. The delegates bowed their heads and then "clasped hands in farewell and went forth each to his place of duty, not knowing the things that should befall us as individuals but with a confidence never shaken by abuse and persecution in certain triumph of our cause."

At the very hour that the delegates were bidding each other good-bye, the spacious home at 92 Lombard Street was in a bustle and stir that was unusual even for that active household. James and Charlotte Forten were giving a farewell dinner party for some of the visiting abolitionists, and they wanted everything to be just right. Charlotte gave a final shine to the mahogany sideboard, polished the tall silver candlesticks, and supervised Margaretta and Sarah in setting the great dining-room table with the fine china and silverware that James had bought for her from an English sea captain.

The enormous roast of beef was brown and fragrant in the oven and the potatoes were being whipped into creamy, buttery mounds when the first of the guests sounded the heavy brass knocker on the front door.

James opened the door to be caught in a bear-hug embrace by William Lloyd Garrison. Close behind him on the marble steps stood the Reverend May; Arthur and Lewis Tappan; Edward Abdy; young James Miller McKim; and John Greenleaf Whittier. About half an hour later Robert Purvis and his wife hurried in. William Deas, the Fortens' youngest child, shyly led the group into the white-paneled dining room and showed each guest where to sit.

The occasion was one that the dinner guests remembered long after that winter evening in 1833. The Reverend May told a friend about it in this way:

> James Forten was evidently a man of commanding mind and well informed. . . . He lived in as handsome a style as anyone could wish to live. I dined at his table

with several members of the Convention and two English gentlemen who had recently come to our country on some philanthropic mission. We were entertained with as much ease and elegance as I could desire to see. . . .

Of course the conversation was for the most part on topics relating to our antislavery conflict. The Colonization scheme came up for consideration, and I shall never forget Mr. Forten's scathing satire: "Why, my great-grandfather was brought to this country as a slave from Africa. My grandfather obtained his own freedom. My father never wore the yoke. . . . [In the Revolution] I was taken prisoner and was made to suffer not a little on board the *Jersey* prison ship.

"I have since lived and labored in a useful employment, have acquired property, and have paid taxes in this city. Here I have dwelt until I am nearly 70 years of age and have brought up and educated a family, as you see, thus far.

"Yet some ingenious gentlemen have recently discovered that I am still an African: that a continent 3,000 miles and more from the place where I was born is my native country. And I am advised to go home. Well, it may be so. Perhaps if I should only be set on the shore of that distant land, I should recognize all I might see there, and run at once to the old hut where my forefathers lived. . .!" His tone of voice, his whole manner sharpened the edge of his sarcasm. It was irresistible. A ripple of laughter swept the table.

At the table sat his motherly wife and his lovely accomplished daughters. . . . I learned from him that their education, evidently of a superior kind, had cost him very much more than it would have done if they had not been denied admission into the best schools of the city.

John Greenleaf Whittier also had lifelong memories of that December dinner. Throughout the evening he had been mostly silent, listening to the conversation with compassion growing in his dark eyes. That night he was unable to sleep

John Greenleaf Whittier, aged 27

until he had set down his thoughts in a poem called, "To The
Daughters of James Forten."

Sisters!—the proud and vain may pass ye by
With rude taunt and cold malicious eye;
Point the pale hand deridingly and slow,
In Scorn's vile gesture at the darker brow;
Curl the pressed lip with sneers which might befit
Some mocking spirit from the nether pit;
Yet, from a heart whence Truth and Love have borne
The last remains of Prejudice and Scorn,
From a warm heart, which, thanks to God, hath felt
Pride's charm to loosen and its iron melt,
Fervent and pure let this frail tribute bear
A Brother's blessing with a Brother's prayer.
And what, my sisters, though upon your brows

The deeper coloring of your kindred glows
Shall I less love the workmanship of Him
Before whose wisdom all our own is dim?
Shall my heart learn to graduate its thrill?
Beat for the White, and for the Black be still?
Let the thought perish, while that heart can feel
The blessed memory of your grateful zeal,
While it can prize the excellence of mind
The chaste demeanor and the state refined,
Still are ye all sisters, meet to share
A Brother's blessing and a Brother's prayer.

On a sparkling, sunny day in mid-April, 1834, Forten the sailmaker stood at the large window in his sail loft that over-looked the Delaware River. For once he was unaware of the white-cloud-winged ships that gracefully rode the shining waves in the distance. His mind was on a circular that Garrison had sent him by special post.

"SHALL THE *LIBERATOR* DIE?" inquired the large print. Smaller print announced that unless the *Liberator's* friends came to its financial rescue, "the paper must cease on the first of July."

Forten frowned as he read the rest of Garrison's communication. The *Liberator's* twenty-three hundred subscriptions were not enough to defray expenses. Of the subscribers, Garrison pointed out:

> ... only one-fourth are white. The paper then belongs emphatically to the people of color—it is their organ. . . . Let them remember that so strong are the prejudices of the whites against it, we cannot at present expect much support from them.
>
> And surely by a very trifling combination of effort and means, the colored population might easily give vigor and stability to the paper. . . . True, they are poor and trodden down; but how can they arise without having a

press to lift up its voice in their behalf? They are poor—but taking the paper will not make them any poorer—it will add to their respectability, their intelligence, and their means. It is for them, therefore, to decide the question SHALL THE LIBERATOR DIE?

For a moment Forten had the thought that it was not fair of Garrison to depend upon the Negroes to support his paper when his white followers were so much better off. Still the sailmaker had to admit that the *Liberator's* influence extended to thousands of persons who did not subscribe to it. Its scathing attacks on the Colonization Society made it difficult for that group to gain a hearing anywhere. In the South its power was so feared that the paper was burned whenever it was found, and *Liberator* readers were frequently beaten and jailed. And the paper did provide a means for free and occasionally enslaved Negroes to raise voices that must otherwise remain silent.

Forten sighed. Garrison and his paper were proving to be more of an expense than he had anticipated, and the cost was not merely that of publishing the *Liberator*. Only recently the editor had returned from a trip to England where he was to raise money for a Manual Labor School for Colored Youth. Although Garrison had been "lionized," the trip had not produced much money for the school, and Garrison's expenses —paid for by Forten and other Negro friends—were heavy. But if the *Liberator* died, what would take its place? Forten knew of no one like Garrison, so brilliant and forceful.

The sailmaker sat down at his desk, and wrote the fiery editor to come to Philadelphia, to stay at his house, and talk over the situation. Garrison's visit was pleasant. Prominent Philadelphia abolitionists such as James and Lucretia Mott visited and had dinner with him at the Fortens. But although they contributed much conversation to the *Liberator's* editor, they gave little money. The result was, as Garrison's sons wrote in after years, that "a significant part of the [*Liberator's*] indebtedness was carried by James Forten." His generosity was called upon again and again. Because of it, the *Liberator* lived to carry on its vehement antislavery campaign until the close of the Civil War.

In 1834, James Forten shared with every Negro in the United States the vexing problem of citizenship. Were the American-born Negroes citizens of the United States or were they not? No one seemed quite sure.

Most people thought that the framers of the Constitution, which made no mention of race or color, never even considered the Negro as a citizen. In 1790, Congress prescribed the mode by which "any alien, being a *white* person, might be naturalized and admitted to the rights of an American citizen." Afterwards Congress repeatedly approved the admission into the Union of states whose constitutions severely restricted the voting rights of free Negroes.

On the other hand, in 1803, when the British were impressing American sailors on the high seas into the British Navy, the House of Representatives resolved to look into the "expediency of granting protection to such American seamen, citizens of the United States, as are free persons of color."

And in Forten's own state of Pennsylvania, legally at least, Negroes could vote. This was possible because, in 1790, when the Pennsylvania Constitution was drawn up, Representative Albert Gallatin, a Swiss immigrant who became one of the nation's leading statesmen, insisted that the word "white" be stricken out before "freeman" as a qualification for voting.

There were other scattered instances of Negroes being regarded as citizens, but since the United States government had not spoken officially on the subject, these separated actions were inconclusive. Apparently when it suited the convenience of the Federal or state government, a Negro could be considered a citizen. Otherwise his claim to the rights and privileges of American citizenship was challenged.

In the light of this background it was not surprising that one hazy afternoon in May, 1834, Forten, who was entertaining four white ministers and the Robert Purvises at tea, kept glancing impatiently out of the window. Where was Mr. Vaux, he thought, fretfully. What news would he bring from the Department of State?

Dusk was casting its shadows when Roberts Vaux, the wealthy, aristocratic, Quaker humanitarian and Controller of the Philadelphia schools, hurried up the Forten walk and into the parlor.

"I've got it. I've got it," he called, smiling, and waving a document at the group. "Thy passport, Robert. And for Harriet, too. Now thee two can be off to Europe."

He handed the paper to Robert Purvis whose voice shook slightly as he read aloud, "To all whom it may concern—to permit safely and freely to pass, Robert Purvis and wife, *citizens of the United States*, and in case of need, to give them all lawful aid and protection." It was signed by John Forsyth, Secretary of State.

The group gathered about the Purvises to congratulate them on the prospect of an exciting European journey, but uppermost in Forten's mind were the words on the passport: Robert Purvis and wife—*citizens of the United States*. To him they stood out as though written in gold—one more piece of evidence that the Government of the United States regarded American Negroes as American citizens.

Forten's feeling of satisfaction was short-lived. As the pleasant spring days of May melted into the heated ones of July, the mad voice of riot again screamed through the land. In New England a mob set upon the gentle poet Whittier, who was speaking against slavery, and threatened his life. In New York City, on the Fourth of July, a white mob broke up an antislavery meeting with fists and clubs. For several days afterward the mobs stormed through the Negro section, clubbing and stoning unoffending colored people, burning their homes, churches, and meetinghouses, and forcing hundreds to flee the city. The homes and store of Arthur and Lewis Tappan were attacked and partially destroyed.

From New York City the disorders quickly spread to Philadelphia, where their uncontrolled violence and their demonstration of a primitive hatred against Negroes and abolitionists of all colors stunned Pennsylvanians of both races.

Gradually, as the hot summer days waned, the temper of the crowds simmered down. By the time the autumn winds bellied the sails on the Delaware, Forten was able to concentrate with pleasure on the accomplishments of his children. James Jr. was becoming known throughout the city as a polished orator, debater, and possessor of a splendid singing voice. Whenever the Union Musical Association of Philadelphia, a Negro group that performed with a Negro orchestra and a Negro conductor, gave its "Annual Concert of Sacred and Instrumental Music," James Jr. was its most acclaimed soloist.

Robert Bridges, his second son, a gifted mathematician, had constructed a fine nine-foot telescope, had ground the lenses for it, and had set them in place. The telescope, to Forten's pride, was on display at the Franklin Institute, a scientific institution.

All the girls were musical, wrote poetry, drew, and painted. All were active in the Female Anti-Slavery Societies that had sprung up in the wake of the American Anti-Slavery Society, which was at first restricted to men. Margaretta served as the secretary of the first of these women's groups, the Philadelphia Female Anti-Slavery Society, of which Lucretia Mott was president. Later, for a general convention of these antislavery women in New York, Sarah Forten wrote this poem:

Lucretia Mott (from a daguerreotype)

We are thy sisters. God has truly said,
That of one blood the nations he has made.
O Christian woman! in a Christian land,
Canst thou unblushing read this great command?
Suffer the wrongs which wring our inmost heart,
To draw one throb of pity on thy part!
Our skins may differ, but from thee we claim
A sister's privilege and a sister's name.

Christmas, 1834, was one of the happiest James could remember. For weeks, Charlotte and the girls had been baking and making cookies and cakes, candies, and pies. Throughout December the spacious house was fragrant with ginger spice and cooking chocolate. For days the pile of brightly wrapped Christmas gifts mounted higher and higher on the large mahogany table near the parlor window, for the Christmas tree had not yet come to America.

On ˙Christmas Day, no matter how much the young people begged to open their gifts and curiously poked the pile of presents, they were not allowed this pleasure until they had returned from Christmas Services at the African Episcopal Church of St. Thomas. It was good for their character to wait, Forten, merry-eyed, would declare when his children protested this edict.

After the opening of the gifts, accompanied by shrieks of surprise and joy, came the "grand dinner." In 1834 it was even grander than usual. Around the great table, heavy with roast goose, large bowls of creamed potatoes and onions, puddings, jellies, and applesauce sat James, Charlotte, the eight Forten children, Robert Purvis, James's widowed sister Abigail and her two children, and four retired sailmakers from the Forten loft who had no real homes of their own.

As soon as the dinner was over, the table was cleared and set with small cakes, nuts, raisins, candies, and an enormous crystal bowl of punch. The Fortens were now ready for their Christmas callers. This year, while the rising hurricane forces of both abolitionism and anti-abolitionism whistled ominously in the distance, an unusual number of white visitors crowded into the holly-decked, candle-lit home at 92 Lombard Street.

Perhaps the outstanding of these were two women, both thirty-two years old. One, Lydia Maria Child of Massachusetts, was the author of the conscience-shaking book *An Appeal in Favor of that Class of Americans called Africans.* The other was the distinguished English author and reformer, Harriet Martineau, who was making a tour of the United States to find out for herself what Americans were really like.

In the parlor, handsome, dark-eyed Mrs. Child paused in front of the gold-framed certificate that the Humane Society had awarded to James Forten for his heroism in rescuing so many persons from drowning. She shook her black curls with admiration.

"How proud you must be of this," she told the tall, erect man at her side.

Forten nodded. "I would not take one thousand dollars for it," he answered warmly.

A short time later when he welcomed the famous Miss Martineau, he managed to hide his surprise. Could this be the imposing lady who had made the intrepid William Lloyd Garrison quake and stammer like a nervous schoolboy when he met her? She stood before him smiling, plump, and rather plain-looking, holding to her ear a large ear-trumpet, for she had been deaf from childhood. Despite her deafness, Miss Martineau carried on a lively conversation in a pleasing voice. James was delighted with her "unaffected, quiet manner, her intelligent, benevolent, and animated voice."

She, too, admired the Humane Society certificate, and her blue eyes sharpened with interest at the books and papers in the Forten library. James saw her stare intently at the Abolitionist journals—he took them all—and at the learned *North American Review* and *The American Quarterly Review* to which he also subscribed.

Harriet Martineau's visit with the Forten family in Philadelphia was one of the events of her American tour that turned her into an active abolitionist for the rest of her life.

16

The Appeal
of Forty Thousand
Citizens

A week after the Christmas party, James and Charlotte celebrated New Year's Day with a visit to their good friends, the Robert Douglasses. James expressed the hope that the summer of 1835 would not bring a return of the disturbances that in previous summers had alarmed thoughtful people of both races.

But his hopes were not fulfilled. As the heated days of the year came on, the voice of the mob screamed again through the land. In a way, the disturbances this time were more frightening, somehow more calculated. The crowds, loitering on the streets during the long daylight hours, seemed to be looking for trouble. And in the meetings of the abolitionists, they found it.

All over the nation, mobs set upon the abolitionists. During one week alone, the *Liberator* reprinted accounts of over one hundred mob attacks on abolitionist speakers throughout the North and West. Forten fervently hoped that Philadelphia would escape the violence agitating other towns and cities, but on the twelfth of July, an unfortunate occurrence set it off.

A former United States Consul to Trinidad, living in Philadelphia, was nearly murdered by his servant, a native African, who attacked him with a hatchet while he slept.

When word of the attack got out, a white mob gathered near the Ex-Consul's house. A large body of policemen was immediately dispatched to the neighborhood, but the angry-looking crowd of men and half-grown boys increased. In the presence of the police the crowd merely muttered among themselves, but, when the police dispersed them, they ran off in small groups toward the Negro section, entered some of the homes, beat up the inmates, destroyed the furniture, and set fire to the houses. When the firemen came to put out the fires, members of the mob cut the hose.

The police arrested as many of the hoodlums as they could find, but they were not able to stamp out the mob spirit. It continued sporadically all over the city with beatings, burnings, and destruction of Negro property.

Even the coming of cool weather, the usual damper of wild behavior, did not calm things down. It was true that many of the abolitionists were irritating in their manner and personalities, with Garrison one of the most irritating of all. In addition, he had a way of putting unpleasant truths before the public eye.

It was not, he declared, simply the poor and uneducated who were attacking the antislavery lecturers. Mobs everywhere were encouraged by manufacturers and merchants who did business with the South, and by banks, insurance companies, bishops, and editors whose prosperity somehow depended upon retaining the good will of the slaveholders.

In October, 1835, Garrison's words were proved right in a way he probably did not like. On the morning of the twenty-first, while he was working in the shabby *Liberator* office and awaiting the visit of a noted English abolitionist, George Thompson, a number of placards and handbills appeared on the Boston streets. They read:

THOMPSON

The Abolitionist! ! ! ! !

That infamous foreign scoundrel THOMPSON will hold forth *this afternoon* at the Liberator office, No. 48 Washington St. The present is a fair opportunity for the friends of the Union to *snake Thompson out*. It will be a contest between the Abolitionists and the friends of the Union. A purse of $100 has been raised by a number of patriotic citizens to reward the individual who shall first lay violent hands on Thompson, so that he may be brought to the tar kettle before dark. Friends of the Union be vigilant!

Boston, Wednesday, 12 O'Clock   October 21, 1835

That was all the mob needed. In the afternoon, about a thousand men, mostly "gentlemen of property and influence," broke into a meeting of the Boston Female Anti-Slavery Meeting, next door to the *Liberator* office, hunting for Thompson who was supposed to be speaking to the women.

Thompson had not yet arrived, but the mob heard that Garrison was in the building. "Garrison! Garrison!" shouted some of the well-dressed mob leaders. "Out with him. Lynch him!" They found the editor, set upon him, and led him through the streets with a rope around his neck, his clothing half-torn from his body. Only jeers came from the thousands who lined the streets watching the spectacle.

Garrison was rescued by the mayor, who surrounded him with police and placed him in jail for his own protection. Deprived of its victim, the mob of "respectable persons" grumbled, shook fists at police, and went home.

Word of the mob attack on Garrison reached James Forten as he was inspecting some special rope from Russia with which to sew his sails. The news, especially that the mob consisted mostly of the supposedly "better class" of people, made him feel old and ill. After all, in less than six months he would be seventy years old. He decided to make his will.

William Lloyd Garrison (from a daguerreotype)

In his lawyer's office he thought carefully about what he wanted to do with his wealth—reported to be over three hundred thousand dollars. First, of course, there was his beloved wife, Charlotte. To her he left the Lombard Street home and all its furnishings. To his widowed sister, Abigail Dunbar, went the house and lot he had bought for her years ago, and also the money for its repair and taxes. A small bequest went to the African Church of St. Thomas and to the Philadelphia Anti-Slavery Society. Charlotte, Robert, and James Jr. were to carry on the business of the sail loft, and the remainder of the estate was to be shared alike by all eight children.

His will made, James went home and allowed himself to be cheered up by the fine oyster pie Charlotte made for his supper and by the songs his children sang for him in the parlor.

In the spring of 1837, Forten read in the newspapers that a special Convention was meeting in the state capital to draw up a new constitution for Pennsylvania.

Emphasis was to be placed upon the qualifications for voting.

The original constitution, drawn up in 1790, had stated: "In elections by the citizens, *every freeman*, of the age of 21 years, having resided in the State two years . . . and within that time paid a State or county tax . . . shall enjoy the rights of an election."

This meant that legally a Negro in Pennsylvania who met the other qualifications could vote. A few did, particularly in the western part of the state. There is no record that James Forten ever voted, yet he probably took pleasure in the belief that he had the right to do so if he wished.

But now in 1837, forty-seven years later, the Pennsylvania legislators were asserting that there was a difference between a freeman and a free man. The fact that a Negro was free did not, many legislators declared, mean that he was a freeman. The term "freeman" went back to an old English law and called for certain acceptances by the community which the Negro did not have. Therefore, the members of this Constitutional Convention argued, the framers of the 1790 Constitution did not intend that the Negro should vote; and now, when the abolitionists were sowing strife across the land, was the time to state clearly in the new Pennsylvania Constitution that Negroes were not eligible to vote.

These legislators had ample precedent for their arguments. Only Maine, New Hampshire, Vermont, Rhode Island, and Massachusetts permitted Negroes actually to vote on equal terms with whites. New Jersey and Connecticut, whose original state constitutions had not mentioned racial distinctions, afterward added the "white only" clause to their voting qualifications. Perhaps it was not surprising that the

Pennsylvania Constitutional Convention voted overwhelmingly to disenfranchise its Negro citizens.

"Indeed the Reform Convention has voted," James commented to Robert Purvis as they discussed the disquieting event, "but the new Constitution still has to be ratified. Perhaps we can yet prevent this."

Both men knew it was a poor time to press for Negro rights. The nation, Philadelphia particularly, was caught in a financial panic. Jobs were scarce, and people generally were in an ugly mood. About the time of the Constitutional Convention, a large crowd gathered in Independence Square to listen to verbal attacks on the banks, which were thought to be at the root of their money troubles. "The excitement was so intense," an observer wrote, "and the crowds so angry that the state officials feared that the mob would pillage and attack the banks. The military was called out in great numbers and dispersed the crowd, but not before some of them vented their misdirected fury upon numbers of hapless Negroes in the area."

These attacks spurred Forten in his fight to prevent the new Constitution's being ratified. In response to a mass meeting of Philadelphia Negroes, he, together with Robert Purvis, in 1838, composed a dramatic pamphlet entitled *Appeal of Forty Thousand Citizens*, threatened with disenfranchisement, to the people of Pennsylvania."

> Fellow Citizens,
> ... Was it the intention of the people of this Commonwealth that the [Reform Convention] should tear up and cast away its first principles? Was it made the business of the Convention to deny "that all men are born equally free," by making political rights depend upon the skin in which a man is born? or to divide what our fathers bled to unite—*Taxation* and *Representation*?
> It is the safeguard of the strongest that he lives under

a government which is obliged to respect the voice of the weakest. When you have taken from an individual his right to vote, you have made the government in regard to him, a mere despotism; and you have taken a step towards making it a despotism to all. . . .

For his part, as his pen scratched on, Forten's feelings ran away with his thoughts, and he wrote of many things that had weighed upon his heart and mind for years.

There was the matter of proving that Negroes were indeed regarded as United States citizens in the early days of the nation. "Proofs might be multiplied," wrote James, quoting again the resolution in the House of Representatives, in 1803, which implied that American seamen, free persons of color, were citizens of the United States.

There was the matter of slavery and the arrest of fugitive slaves which Forten believed was behind the move to take away the vote from the Negro:

> . . . This is not the first time that northern statesmen have bowed the knee to the dark spirit of slavery, but it is the first time they have bowed so low! Is Pennsylvania, which abolished slavery in 1780 and enfranchised her tax-paying citizens in 1790 now, in 1838, to get upon her knees and repent of her humanity, to gratify those who disgrace the very name of American Liberty, by holding our brethren as goods and chattels? We freely acknowledge our brotherhood to the slave, and our interest in his welfare. Is this a crime for which we should be ignominiously punished? . . . .
>
> [The slaveholders] see in everything which fortifies our rights, an obstacle to the recovery of their fugitive property. Need we inform you that every colored man in Pennsylvania is exposed to be arrested as a fugitive from slavery? . . . . Thus may a free-born citizen of Pennsylvania be arrested, tried without counsel, jury, or power to call

Robert Purvis (from a daguerreotype)

witnesses, condemned by a single man and carried across Mason and Dixon's line, within the compass of a single day....

Imagine your own wives and children to be trembling at the aproach of every stranger, lest their husbands and fathers should be dragged into slavery ... worse than death.

Both Forten and Purvis were aware that the Negro suffered from what today we would call a "poor image." Without thinking, many white people declared that he was lazy, shiftless, and ignorant, and that he had no desire to improve himself.

Forten had long since stopped getting angry when he heard such statements. What was the use? Most people saw only what they wished to see. But why not, Purvis urged, include in the *Appeal* the statistics gathered for the petition of 1832? These would prove that the free Negroes not only were *not* a burden upon the public treasury but that they actually *added* to the prosperity of the whites.

To the figures that showed what Pennsylvania Negroes were doing for themselves educationally, Forten added a new feature—libraries. "We have among ourselves," he wrote, "two public libraries consisting of about 800 volumes, besides 8,333 volumes in private libraries."

And then, as always, the sailmaker's mind returned to the fact that Negroes had been a part of the American scene from the earliest days of the nation. He added, with some bitterness:

> Our fathers shared with yours the trials and perils of the wilderness. . . . we are not intruders here, nor were our ancestors. Surely you ought to bear as unrepiningly the evil consequences of your fathers' guilt, as we those of our fathers' misfortune. . . .
>
> We would have the right of suffrage only as the reward of industry and worth. We care not how high the qualification be placed. All we ask is that no man shall be excluded on account of his *color*, that the same rule shall be applied to all. . . .
>
> Firm upon our Pennsylvania Bill of Rights, and trusting in a God of truth and justice, we lay our claim before you, with the warning that no amendments of the present Constitution can compensate for the loss of its foundation principle of equal rights, nor for the conversion into enemies of 40,000 friends.

As Chairman of the Committee, Robert Purvis signed the *Appeal*. More and more now would the aging sailmaker turn over his public activities on behalf of his people to his son-in-law.

After the pamphlet was distributed throughout the state, Forten and Purvis began the long months of waiting to see what effect the *Appeal of Forty Thousand Citizens* would have upon the people of Pennsylvania. It had little. In October, 1838, the new Constitution, which said that only *white freemen* could vote, was ratified. After that, no Negro voted in Pennsylvania until 1873.

17

"Death of an Excellent Man"

The news that the vote had officially been taken away from his people threw Forten the sailmaker into a despondent mood. Instead of going to his sail loft he sat at home and stared gloomily through the large parlor window at the dreary fall day outside. Suddenly the knocker sounded at the front door. Charlotte set her knitting down on the marble-topped table and let in the visitor—John Greenleaf Whittier.

James rose to greet him. Years later, James's granddaughter, the well-known poet and teacher, Charlotte Forten, would write of Whittier, "In these dark hours, the noble young poet of freedom came to him, and his indignant protest against wrong, his loving companionship, his warm, outspoken sympathy, were a source of unspeakable consolation and hope."

Now the two men moved their chairs close to the cheery fire James Jr. had started in the fireplace. They began to talk about the blow that had been dealt to the principle of democracy in the state.

"The vote decision is not surprising," said Whittier in his mild, clear voice. "We should have seen it coming. Consider the matter of Pennsylvania Hall."

"Pennsylvania Hall." James shuddered. The affair was still a nightmare to him.

It had begun in 1837, when the Abolitionists and other liberal groups, who were having trouble getting meeting places, determined to build a hall of their own. With forty thousand dollars, collected chiefly from their own group, the Abolitionists built a splendid marble building on 6th Street "dedicated to the rights of free discussion." The first floor of Pennsylvania Hall housed lecture and committee rooms and an office for the *Pennsylvania Freeman*, the weekly paper that Whittier had taken over from the aging Benjamin Lundy. The second floor contained the auditorium, magnificent with elegant gas fixtures and blue plush seats for three thousand people. Unquestionably Pennsylvania Hall was one of the finest meeting places in the nation.

On Dedication Day, the fourteenth of May, 1838, it was announced that the hall had not been erected for antislavery purposes alone, and everything went smoothly. The afternoon lectures were devoted to essays on social and scientific subjects by the staid Philadelphia Lyceum Society. The evening was given over to a Temperance Meeting.

The program the following afternoon included a temperance lecture, debates on "Indian Wrongs," "Colonization," and scientific essays by the Philadelphia Lyceum. Quiet prevailed in Philadelphia. Then, on the evening of May 15, the Abolitionists held a meeting. Forten, his sons Robert and James Jr., his daughters Sarah and Margaretta, and the Robert Purvises, all of whom had attended earlier meetings, thought nothing of going in as they had before with their white friends, William Lloyd Garrison, the Motts, and Maria Chapman, a Boston abolitionist.

But if they attached no importance to their joining their white friends in Pennsylvania Hall, thousands of Philadelphians looked upon the matter differently. One observer of the time described it this way:

> During these two days [May 14 and 15] the Hall was crowded, and on the streets leading to it were throngs of persons pressing towards the building. Among these were people of color, admitted freely and without distinction, and sat among the audience, not being particularly

assigned to any reserved space set aside for "people of color." Among the throngs passing along the streets white abolitionists and black walked frequently in company with others and on friendly terms. It was reported that white men and black women and white women and black men walked arm in arm. This angered the people. A rising hostility against the building and its occupants began to be manifested. . . .

In different parts of the city, written placards were posted. "A convention to effect immediate emancipation of the slaves throughout the country is in session in this city," the placards read, "and it is the duty of citizens who entertain a proper respect for the Constitution of the Union and the right of property *to interfere*."

"Assemble at Pennsylvania Hall tomorrow morning [May 16] the placards urged, and "demand immediate dispersion of said convention."

Apparently none of the abolitionists, including the Forten and Purvis families, paid attention to these threats. The next morning, Sarah, Margaretta, and Harriet attended the "Anti-Slavery Convention of American Women." In the evening, Forten and his sons and Robert Purvis accompanied them to the Abolitionist meeting, at which Garrison, Maria Chapman, and Abby Kelly from Boston were to speak.

They found the streets near the Hall thronged with hoodlums who shouted insults as the abolitionists walked by. Some ruffians even ran into the auditorium and hooted at the speakers who were seated on the platform. Others threw stones from the street, breaking the windows and showering speakers and audience with glass.

The managers of Pennsylvania Hall appealed to Mayor Swift for police protection for themselves and their property during meetings yet to be held.

"Give up the meetings," the Mayor begged. "I cannot guarantee you protection."

"But it is our right as citizens to hold these meetings," the abolitionists protested. "We will not give them up."

The next night, May 17, the mob that gathered near Pennsylvania Hall was larger and uglier. Speakers, spewing hate, urged the crowd to "destroy, destroy." Within the Hall the managers, growing alarmed, decided to close the building and give the key to the Mayor. This time the Mayor tried to reason with the throng, and begged the people to go home. Some did, but hundreds of others crowded in.

Suddenly the street lights in the area went out. Men with long pieces of wood battered against the front door. As they were pounding against the door, the Mayor, surrounded by police, pushed his way through the crowd. The mob then set upon the police and knocked some of them to the ground. Other officers managed to escape and make their way into the main auditorium. The mob had got there first. A bonfire blazed on the speaker's platform. Two smaller fires flamed on the sides of the great room. To make the fire blaze hotter, the ruffians had broken the gas pipes on the wall. The dangerous leaking gas fumes and the leaping flames forced the police to withdraw.

They barely got out with their lives, for the mob rampaging on the first floor had already set fire to the antislavery books and pamphlets, to Whittier's papers and newspaper equipment. The flames raced up the stairway with a roar. Firemen, hampered and threatened by the mob, were unable to do anything except play their hose on the adjoining property.

Forten, standing across the street with the Motts, watched in dismay as the whole front of the building crumbled into ruin, and the interior crashed into a blackened rubble which threw off showers of sparks. In a few minutes Pennsylvania Hall, three days old, the "beautiful temple consecrated to Liberty," was lost.

Even the burning of Pennsylvania Hall did not satisfy the mob. The next evening a rabble attacked the Quaker-run Shelter for Colored Orphans and set fire to it. Again the firemen appeared, and again the hoodlums tried to prevent their saving the property. But this time ordinary citizens, sickened by the mob behavior, went to the aid of the police and firemen. The orphanage was saved, and the ruffians were jailed.

Memories of the savage attack on the orphanage so distressed Forten that he begged Whittier to speak of happier things.

"Of course," Whittier answered sympathetically, "but one thing I've been wanting to ask you. Whatever happened to Garrison that night? One moment I saw him trying to save some books from the antislavery office, and the next moment he was gone."

"Didn't you know?" Forten answered, surprised. "My son-in-law [Robert Purvis] was afraid the mob would kill him, so he grabbed him, pushed him into a closed carriage, and drove him full speed out of town."

As the year 1838 wound on to its close, Forten the sailmaker remarked to Robert Purvis that Philadelphia should no longer be known as the "City of Brotherly Love." Instead it should be called "Mob City!" "No other Northern city treats its colored people so badly," he exclaimed angrily. "We are mobbed. Insults of all kind are heaped on us. We find most places of public entertainment, halls, and lecture rooms closed against us."

Purvis nodded understandingly. "Yes, but still *they* continue to come here for help."

"They" were the runaway slaves. More and more of them were reaching Philadelphia, only forty miles from the slave borders, hoping someone would help them to freedom.

In earlier years, aiding a runaway slave had been simpler. He was fed, clothed, told to follow the North Star, and sent on alone to the next town, usually with directions to some Quaker family there. Once away from his master's neighborhood, he was seldom pursued. But now things were different.

Although a larger number of slaves succeeded in escaping, their way was increasingly difficult. More persons were engaged in tracking them down and returning them to their masters. Most abolitionists were known, and their enemies watched carefully to make sure they harbored no fugitives. If they did, these enemies promptly notified the authorities.

But still the dark-skinned runaways came to Pennsylvania. William Still, of Underground Railroad fame, described them this way: "They crept up creek beds, through swamps, over the hills in the dark of night, wading in streams to throw off bloodhounds. They hid in barns, cellars, churches, woodsheds, and caves, and rode to safety in wagons with . . . false bottoms," made especially for this purpose.

Gradually certain places became known to the runaways as "way-stations" on an Underground Railroad to freedom. The persons whose homes were used as these stations were called "Station-Masters." Two of the earliest of these Station-Masters were James Forten and Robert Purvis. Purvis, whose large farm at Byberry served as the hideout for hundreds of fugitive slaves, is credited with being the chief founder of the Underground Railroad, but seventy-three-year-old James Forten was equally active in the movement.

His spacious home on Lombard Street was always filled with people. The Philadelphia city directory listed twenty-two persons as permanently living there. If three or four more daily gathered around the large dining-room table, who could say definitely that the visitors did not belong there, or were not invited guests?

In 1839, Forten and Purvis organized the Vigilant Committee of Philadelphia whose purpose was to guide and fi-

nance escaping slaves, mainly to Canada. The first Minute
Book of the Vigilant Committee in 1839 shows a number of
entries in James's handwriting:

> Case 31: Woman from Virginia, emancipated on
> condition of going to Liberia. Sent to Byberry. Expense,
> $3.00.
> Case 40: Eight persons from Virginia. A very in-
> teresting family. Sent to Canada, accompanied by the
> agent.
> Cases 2 and 3: Two men, one sent to the Committee
> by Wm. Whipper. Col'd from Virginia, light complexion,
> an interesting young man sent to Morrisville from thence
> to New York for Canada. The other was employed some
> few weeks at Fallingstone, since left for Canada. The
> expense attending these two cases was $4.83.

The Vigilant Committee and the Underground Railroad
were Forten's chief activities in his last years. Outwardly he
seemed to have changed but little since he was twenty-five.
"He has," said one man who had known him for fifty years,
"the same manly look, the same elastic tread, the same virtu-
ous sentiments, and the same lofty and enthusiastic patriotism
as when first I grasped his hand."

But inwardly, Forten was different. The defeat of the
Appeal of Forty Thousand Citizens had shaken him badly.
And although, as they had done in former years, members of
the Pennsylvania Legislature and other prominent persons
came to sit with him in his parlor, obviously admiring and
interested in his story, somehow their voices were soundless
to him now. It was as though their lips moved but they said
nothing. Sometimes he gazed at these callers intently, curiously, wondering if any of them could speak as had Pennsylvania's great humanitarians, Penn and Franklin, Benezet and
Rush.

These visitors seemed unaware of his thoughts. They
went away remarking, as white visitors always did, upon his

"polish," his "gentlemanliness," his "fine appearance," his "excellent" mind.

In February, 1842, James worried his family by going to bed and staying there for more than a week. In all his seventy-five years, he had never been ill for more than two days at a time. But now he lay quietly, reading his Bible and quoting favorite poems to his beloved five-year-old granddaughter, Charlotte, Robert's child.

On the twenty-fourth of the month he asked his wife and his eight children to come and sit by him. Taking Charlotte's hand he said, "I am going now. I feel a peace that passeth all understanding."

Just before his speech failed, he asked that his love be given to all his abolition friends, "especially to Garrison."

He was buried several days later in the graveyard of the African Church of St. Thomas—the last of the original members of the first Negro church in America.

The newspapers took especial notice of his death. Under the heading "Death of an Excellent Man," the *North American and Daily Advertiser* said, "We learn that James Forten, an old and highly respectable colored citizen died yesterday morning. Mr. Forten has for many years been the leading sailmaker in this city. His strict integrity and great amenity of manners made him many warm friends among our best citizens. Mr. Forten, when a boy, was taken prisoner by the British whilst cruising in one of our vessels and confined in the celebrated *Jersey* prison ship during part of the Revolutionary War. He was established in business by Thomas Willing and afterward patronized by Willing and Francis. . . ."

William Lloyd Garrison wrote to one of the Douglass family: "He was a man of rare qualities and worthy to be held in veneration to the end of time. He was remarkable for his virtues, his self respect. . . . An example like his is of inestimable value, especially in the mighty struggle now taking place between liberty and slavery—reason and prejudice."

The *Maryland Colonization Journal* commented, "We had a slight acquaintance with Mr. Forten, and had reason to think very highly of him as a man of honour, integrity, and true respectability. We regret most deeply, however, that he should have been so decided an opponent of the colonization cause, and we believe he has been mainly instrumental in enlisting the whole mass of the coloured population of our cities in a crusade against it. He no doubt was actuated by the best intuitions, based upon the hope of shortly seeing his brethren admitted to all the rights and privileges of citizenship in the United States. But he lived not to see that day, and we fear the Simeon is not yet born that will."

The *Philadelphia Public Ledger* commented that Forten's funeral "was one of the largest funeral processions we ever saw—numbering from three to five thousand persons, white and colored, male and female, about one-half white—to an extent never before witnessed in this city. . . . Among the white portion were seen some of our wealthiest merchants and shippers, captains of vessels and others. . . . The deceased had the reputation of being strictly honest, liberal to a fault, of unvaryingly kind and courteous demeanor."

A visiting Englishman, Sir Charles Lyell, like the editor of the *Ledger*, was impressed with Forten's generosity. "He had made his fortune as a sailmaker," Sir Charles wrote, "and is said to have been worth at one time 60,000 pounds, but to have lost a great part of his riches by lending money with more generosity than prudence."

Forten the sailmaker would have smiled at Sir Charles's choice of words. Prudence was not a quality he even considered when he gave away thousands of dollars to help members of his race, free and slave alike. In April, 1842, when an inventory of his estate was made, it was found that his fortune had dwindled from three hundred thousand dollars to a little over sixty-seven thousand dollars.

After he was gone, louder and louder grew the voices of violence and unreason. Fainter and fainter came the voices of humanity and justice which had spoken so clearly in the first years of the Republic. Gradually the clamorous fury of the abolitionists, the angry protests of the slaveholders, the arguments of the colonizationists, the pleas of the free Negroes, and the whimpers of the slaves all merged into one tremendous babble that made it impossible for reasonable men to meet on common ground and solve the great problem.

And then nineteen years later, in 1861, the babble itself disappeared into a louder, infinitely more tragic rhythm, the tramp, tramp, tramp of marching feet.

Forten the sailmaker was not there to hear this dreadful sound, or to witness the long and savage war that brought emancipation to his people. But if he had been, his ear would have caught, through the tumult, the voices that still spoke of justice to the Negro people—clearly, and with hope.

Bibliography

Material about James Forten is very scattered. Known during his lifetime for his modesty, the Philadelphia sailmaker made little of his achievements and left no autobiography to aid a present-day biographer. The most valuable source of collected information that I found was an article "James Forten: Forgotten Abolitionist," by Dr. Ray A. Billington, in the *Negro History Bulletin* for November, 1949, which, with its references, served as the springboard for my own research.

Other helpful sources consulted were:

BIOGRAPHIES AND PERSONAL REMINISCENCES

Abdy, Edward. *Journal of a Residence and Tour in the United States of North America from April 1833–October 1835.* London, 1835.

Brooke, George. *Friend Anthony Benezet.* Philadelphia, 1937.

Child, Lydia M. *The Freedmen's Book.* Boston, 1865.

Cooper, Anna J. *Personal Recollections of the Grimke Family.* Private Printing, 1951.

Dring, Thomas. *Recollections of the Jersey Prison Ship.* Providence, 1829.

Fox, Ebeneezer. *The Revolutionary Adventures of Ebeneezer Fox.* Boston, 1839.

Garrison, W.P. and Francis. *William Lloyd Garrison, 1805–1879,* vols. 1–3. Boston, 1894.

Gloucester, Reverend S. H. *Discourse.* Philadelphia, April 17, 1842.

Griggs, E. L. *Thomas Clarkson, The Friend of Slaves.* London, 1936.

Grimke, A. H. *William Lloyd Garrison.* New York, 1891.

Hallowell, Anna D. *James and Lucretia Mott, Life and Letters.* Boston, 1884.

Lascelles, Edward. *Granville Sharp and the Freedom of the Slaves.* London, 1928.

Lyell, Sir Charles. *Travels in North America in the Years 1841–1842.* London, 1855.

May, Samuel J. *Some Recollections of the Anti-Slavery Conflict.* Boston, 1869.

Nell, W. C. *Colored Patriots of the Revolution.* Boston, 1855.

Payne, Daniel A. *Recollections of Seventy Years.* Nashville, 1888.

Purvis, Robert. *Remarks on the Life and Character of James Forten.* Philadelphia, 1842.

Ritter, Abraham. *Philadelphia and Her Merchants.* Philadelphia, 1860.

Sherwood, H. N. "Paul Cuffe," *Journal of Negro History.* April, 1923.

Spring Gardner. *Memoir of Mills.* Boston, 1829.

Vaux, Roberts. *Memoirs of the Life of Anthony Benezet.* Philadelphia, 1817

Warner, Oliver. *William Wilberforce.* London, 1962.

Wilson, Joseph W. *Sketches of the Higher Classes of Colored Society in Philadelphia.* Philadelphia, 1841.

HISTORICAL AND GENERAL BACKGROUND

Aptheker, Herbert. *A Documentary History of the Negro People in the United States.* New York, 1951.

Cromwell, John W. *The Negro in American History.* Washington, 1914.

Douglass, William. *Annals of the First African Church in the United States of America.* Philadelphia, 1862.

DuBois, W. E. B. *The Philadelphia Negro.* Philadelphia, 1899.

Fox, Early. *The American Colonization Society.* Baltimore, 1919.

Franklin, John Hope. *From Slavery to Freedom—A History of American Negroes.* New York, 1956.

Frazier, E. Franklin. *The Free Negro Family.* Nashville, 1932.

Garrison, William Lloyd. *Thoughts on African Colonization.* Boston, 1832.

Hughes, Langston and Meltzer, Milton. *A Pictorial History of the Negro in America.* New York, 1956.

Kipping, Robert. *Sails and Sailmaking.* London, 1861.

Litwack, Leon. *North of Slavery, The Negro in the Free States, 1790–1860.* Chicago, 1961.

Livermore, George. *Negroes as Slaves, Citizens, and Soldiers.* Boston, 1863.

Porter, Dorothy B. "Early Manuscript Letters Written by Negroes," *Journal of Negro History.* April, 1839.

Quarles, Benjamin. *The Negro in the American Revolution.* Chapel Hill, 1961.

Scharf, J. Thomas and Westcott, Thompson. *History of Philadelphia.* Philadelphia, 1884.

Turner, Edward R. *The Negro in Pennsylvania, 1639–1861.* Washington, 1911.

Watson, J. F. *Annals of Philadelphia, 1831–1857.* Philadelphia.

Woodson, Carter G. *The Negro in Our History.* Washington, 1961.

NEWSPAPERS AND OTHER PERIODICALS

Annals of Congress. 6th Congress, 1st session.

Freedom's Journal. New York, 1827.

Hazard's Register of Pennsylvania. Philadelphia, 1828–1838.

Journal of Negro History. Washington, 1917–1967. Valuable information is scattered through many volumes.

The Liberator. Boston, 1831–1842.

Negro History Bulletin. Washington, 1937–1967. Valuable information is scattered through many volumes.

Old South Leaflets, vol. 14. "The Anti-Slavery Convention, 1833." Boston, 1900.

MISCELLANEOUS SOURCES

Forten, Charlotte. Unpublished Diary, Moorland Collection, Howard University.

Forten, James. *Letters of a Man of Color.* Philadelphia, 1813.

Philadelphia City Directories. 1800–1843.

Purvis, Robert. *Appeal of Forty Thousand Citizens.* Philadelphia, 1838.

——*Minute Book of the Vigilant Committee.* Philadelphia, 1838–1839.

Scrapbooks of Philadelphia Negroes in Moorland Collection, Howard University.

Whittier, John G. "To The Daughters of James Forten," in *The Independent,* November, 1906.

SPECIAL COLLECTIONS

Cuffe Papers, New Bedford Public Library.

Garrison Papers, Boston Public Library.

Samuel J. May Anti-Slavery Collection, Cornell University.

Mott Papers, Friends Historical Society, Swarthmore College.

One further note: My research disclosed little description of Benezet's School for colored children. The incident of the mouse in Chapter I—so revealing of Benezet's character and methods—was therefore taken from the reminiscences of some of his white pupils.

Index